MATHS REINFORCERS

- Algebra
- Statistics
- Probability

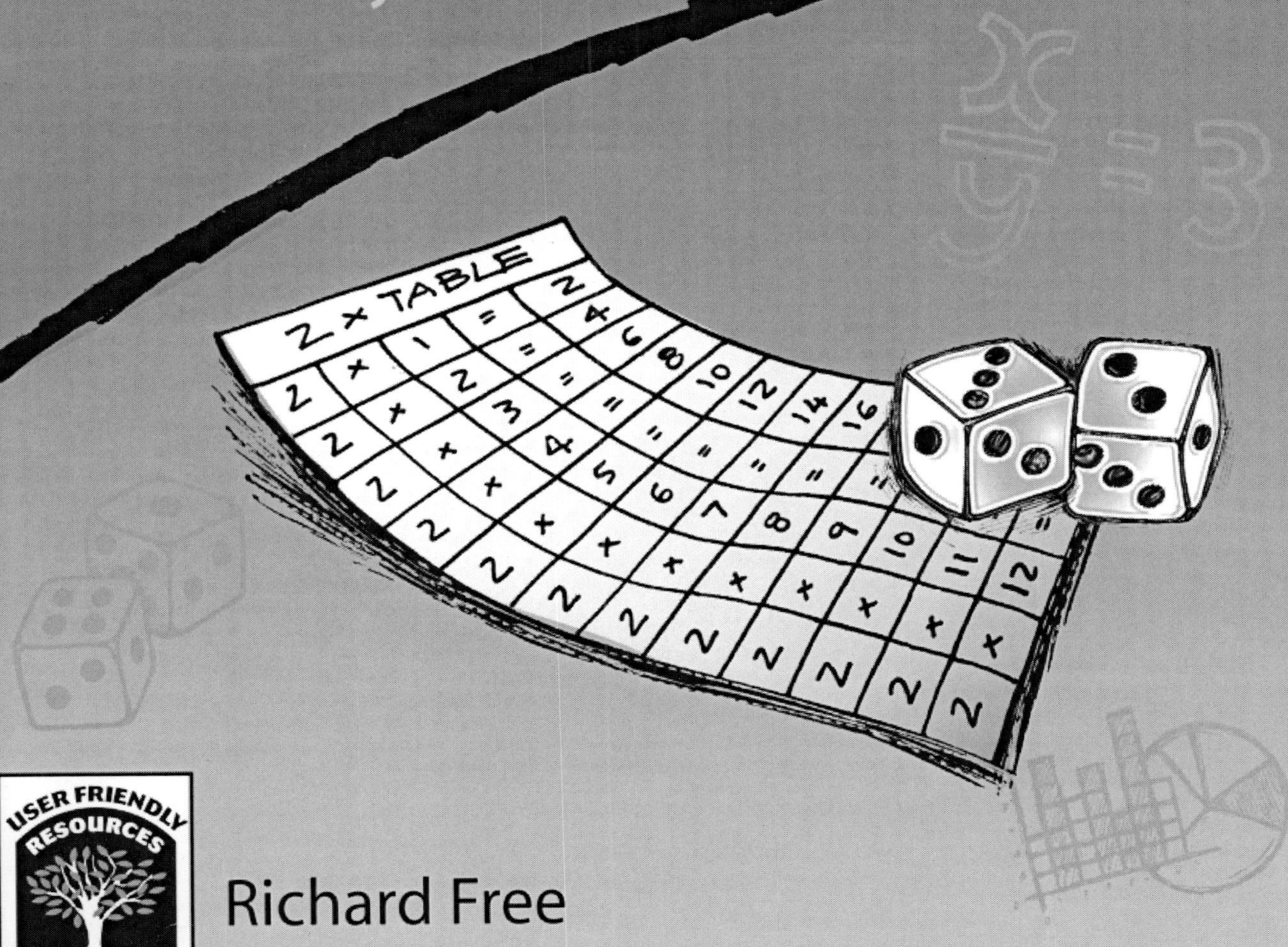

Richard Free

USER FRIENDLY RESOURCES
EDUCATIONAL PUBLISHERS
www.userfr.com

Published by User Friendly Resources. Book No. 439D

TITLE

Book Name: Maths Reinforcers: Algebra, Statistics and Probability
Book Number: 439D
ISBN Number: ISBN 1-86968-219-X
Published: 2006

AUTHOR

Richard Free

ACKNOWLEDGEMENTS

User Friendly Resources wishes to acknowledge the work of the following people in the various stages of publishing this resource.

Designer: Loren Mckey
Illustrator: Geraldine Sloane
Editor: Pauline Scanlan

PUBLISHERS

User Friendly Resources.

c/- AFM Ltd	Australian Office	New Zealand Office
Units 8,9,10, Parkside	P.O. Box 914	P.O. Box 1820
Laughton,	Mascot, NSW 2020	Christchurch
Shortgate Lane	Ph: 1800-553-890	Ph: 0508-500-393
East Sussex BN8 6DG	Fax: 1800-553-891	Fax: 0508-500-399
Ph: 0845-450-7502		
Fax: 0845-450-7501		

WEBSITE

View all our resources at www.userfr.com

CONTENTS

CONTENTS CONTINUED

INTRODUCTION

The worksheets in this resource book have been designed to support students in developing their understanding of the following areas of Mathematics:

- Algebra
- Statistics
- Probability

The book provides a series of worksheets on each topic along with answers on a copy of the original worksheet, which makes it easy for students to mark their own work.

The worksheets excel at building and reinforcing basic skills. They build skills step by step and work towards understanding from a variety of angles, using many everyday examples. The intention is to give students the best chance of understanding basic concepts and mastering basic skills.

The worksheets are suitable to be used:

- As quick 'warm–ups' for maths sessions.
- To provide practice for groups of students while the teacher is released to work with individuals.
- As a targeted activities for particular students who need assistance in basic skills.
- For homework.
- And, of course, for regular work building and reinforcing skills in the classroom.

Many of the worksheets can be cut into fours, providing 'quick questions' when a short task is appropriate, for example at the start or end of a lesson, or for a quick revision task to be done at home. However, the quick questions on one page are related to each other, so they may also be used as parts of a longer activity by keeping them together.

The tasks have been designed for students of various ages working with basic skills. At higher levels teachers will find them particularly useful for students who need extra learning support.

The **Maths Reinforcers** series also includes books on:

- Number Skills
- Fractions, Decimals and Percentages
- Ratio and Proportion, Mass, Time, Plane Shapes, Length, Area and Volume

Stick Rules

Use matchsticks to construct the shape patterns below. Fill in the tables. For each table, work out the rule that gives the number of matches to make each shape. The first one has been done for you.

1.

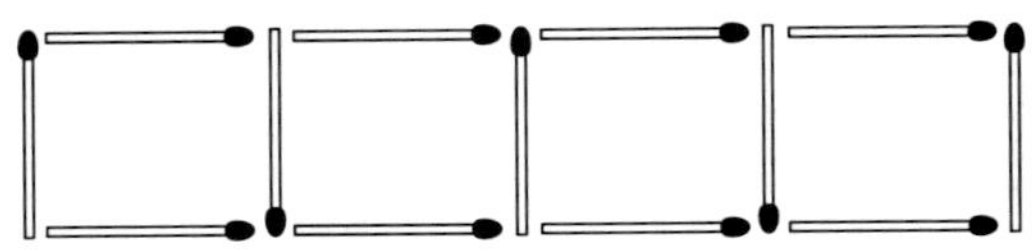

Number of squares	1	2	3	4	5	6
Number of matches	4	7	10	13	16	19
Number of matches = **3 x the number**						
of squares + 1						

2.

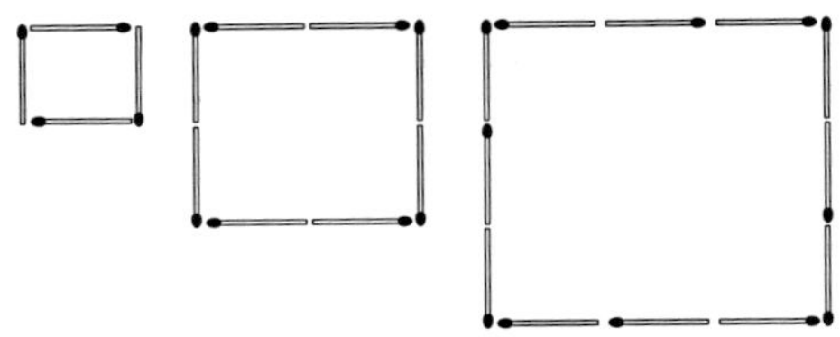

Length of side of square						
Number of matches						
Number of matches =						

3.

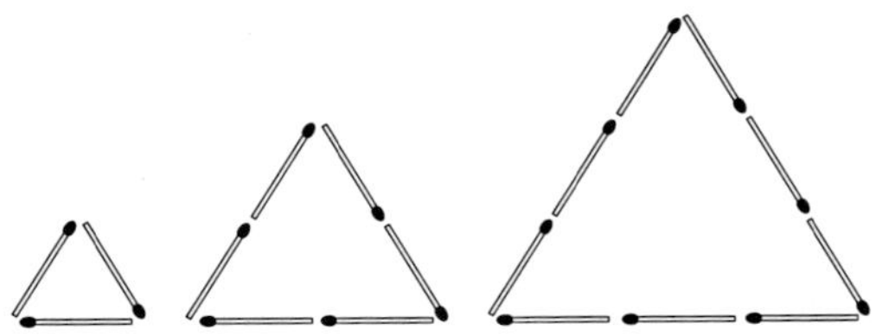

Length of side of triangle						
Number of matches						
Number of matches =						

4.

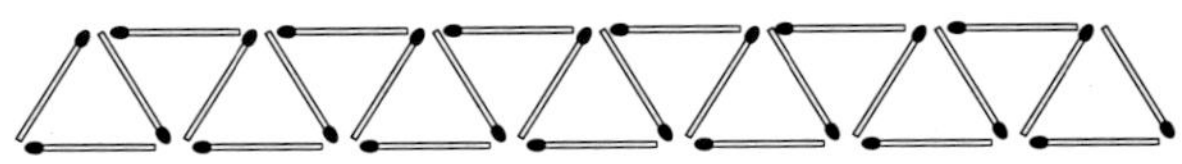

Number of triangles						
Number of matches						
Number of matches =						

5.

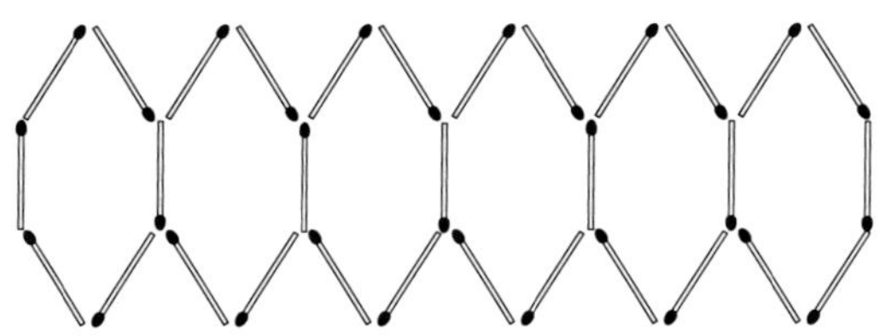

Number of hexagons						
Number of matches						
Number of matches =						

6.

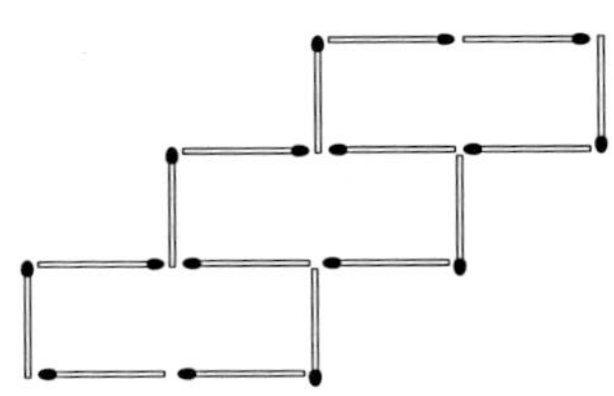

Number of rectangles						
Number of matches						
Number of matches =						

7.

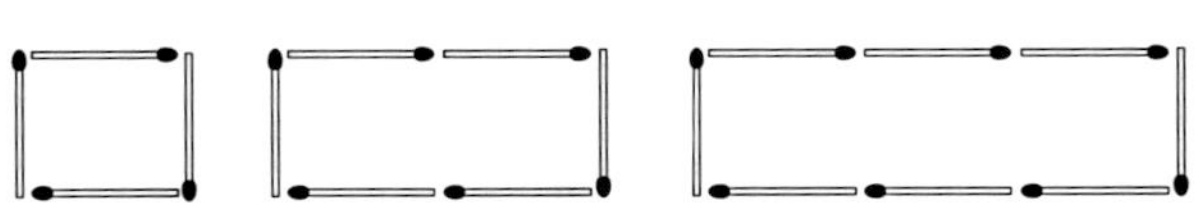

Length of side of rectangle						
Number of matches						
Number of matches =						

8. Design your own pattern

Finding Rules to Work Out Perimeter

Measure the length of each side of the shapes below and work out the perimeter of each. Then complete the rule.

1.

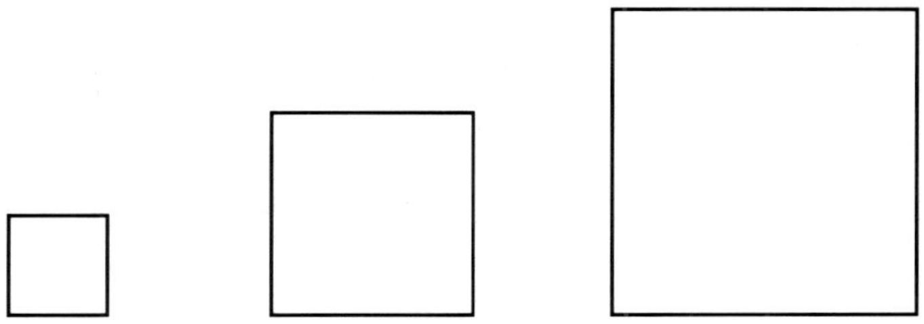

Side _____ Perimeter _____

Side _____ Perimeter _____

Side _____ Perimeter _____

Rule:

The perimeter is _____ the length of 1 side.
What length is the perimeter if each side is 22 cm?
Perimeter is _____ cm.

2.

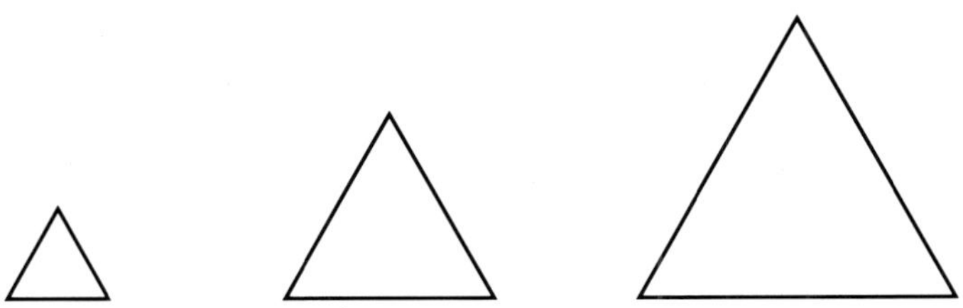

Side _____ Perimeter _____

Side _____ Perimeter _____

Side _____ Perimeter _____

Rule:

The perimeter is _____ the length of 1 side.
What length is the perimeter if each side is 41 cm?
Perimeter is _____ cm.

3.

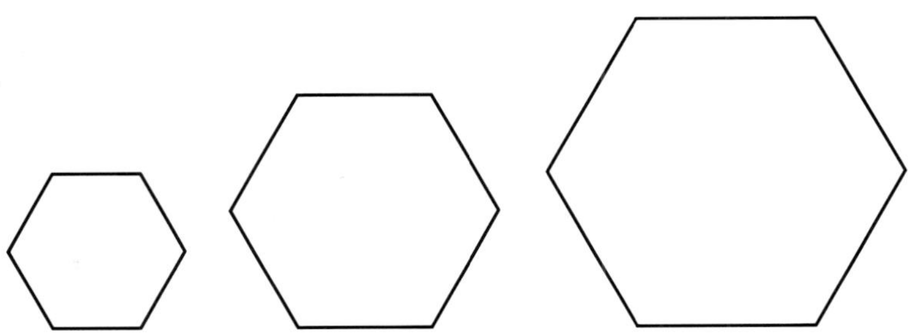

Side _____ Perimeter _____

Side _____ Perimeter _____

Side _____ Perimeter _____

Rule:

The perimeter is _____ the length of 1 side.
What length is the perimeter if each side is 67 cm?
Perimeter is _____ cm.

List some items here that have all sides of equal length.

Square Window Rule: **Perimeter is 4 x the length of one side**

_____ Rule: _____

_____ Rule: _____

_____ Rule: _____

A Rule to Build a Garden Path

Draw slabs around the shaded areas of garden below. Work out a relationship between the length of the side of the garden and the number of slabs needed to go all around the garden. The third garden has been done for you.

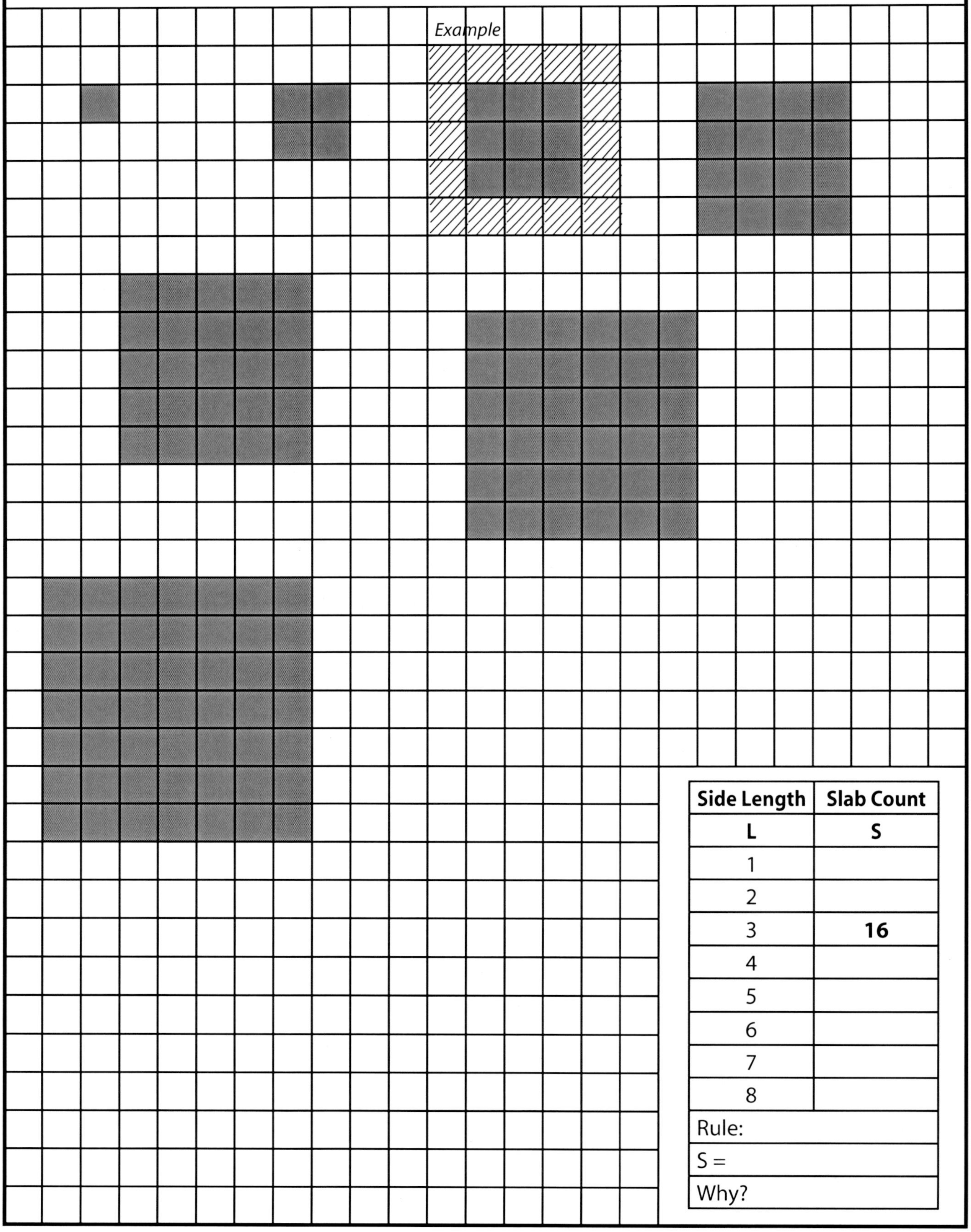

Side Length	Slab Count
L	**S**
1	
2	
3	**16**
4	
5	
6	
7	
8	
Rule:	
S =	
Why?	

More Rules for Building Paths

Draw slabs around the shaded areas of garden below, as in the example. If L is the length of each garden, work out haw many slabs (S) you need to pave around each garden. What is the rule for finding the number of slabs in each of the three situations?

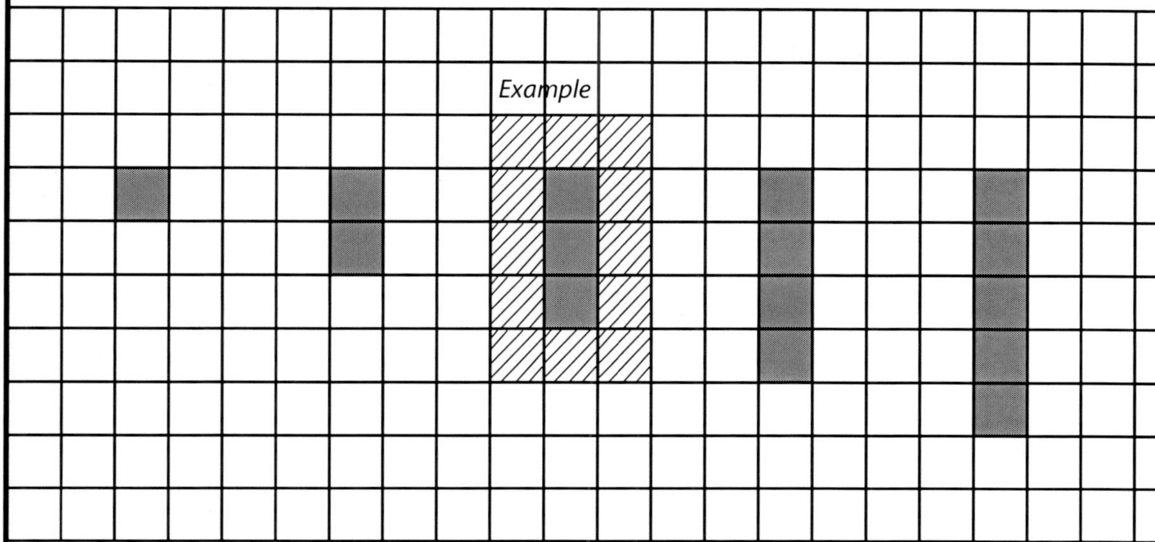

L	S
1	
2	
3	**12**
4	
5	
Rule:	

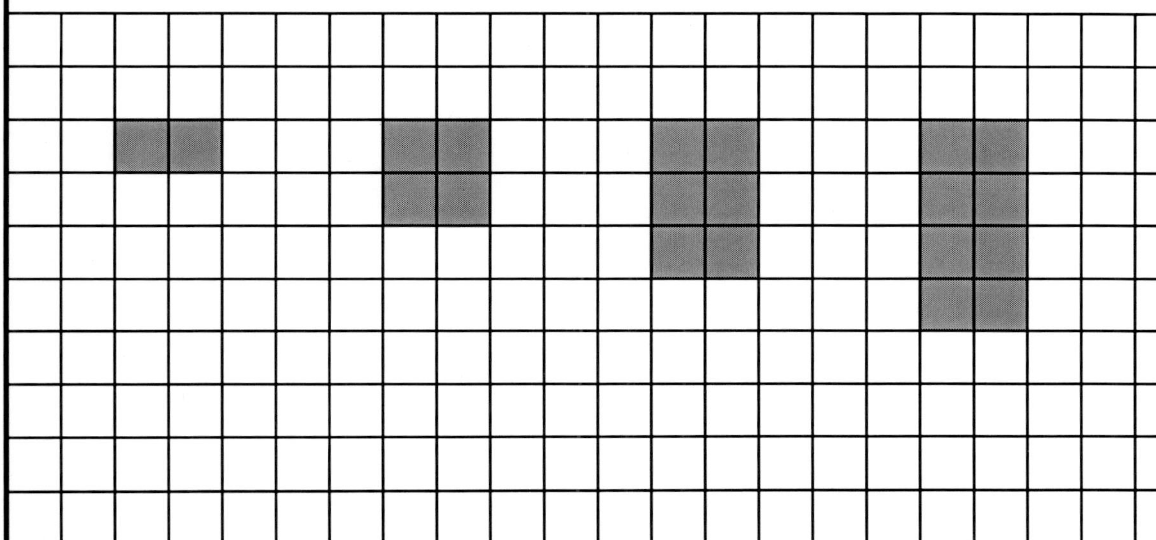

L	S
1	
2	
3	
4	
Rule:	

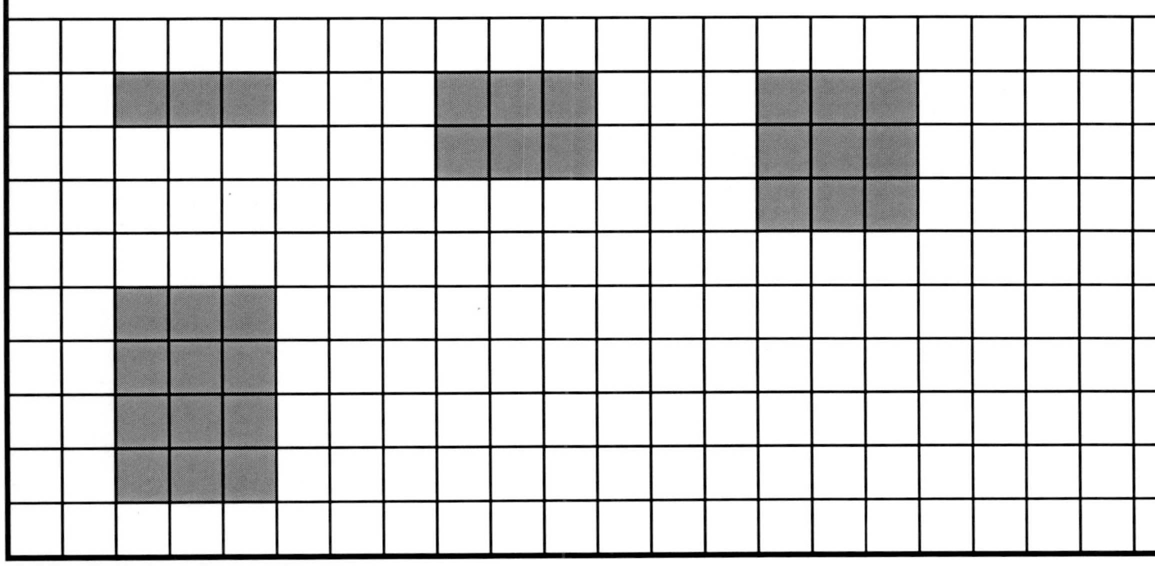

L	S
1	
2	
3	
4	
Rule:	

Searching for Rules with Circles

Use a ruler to connect every point (x) on each circle to every other point (x) on the circle. Record how many lines you draw in each circle. Think of a rule that lets you find how many lines you need to connect any number of points. (This is hard!)

3 points need
__3__ lines

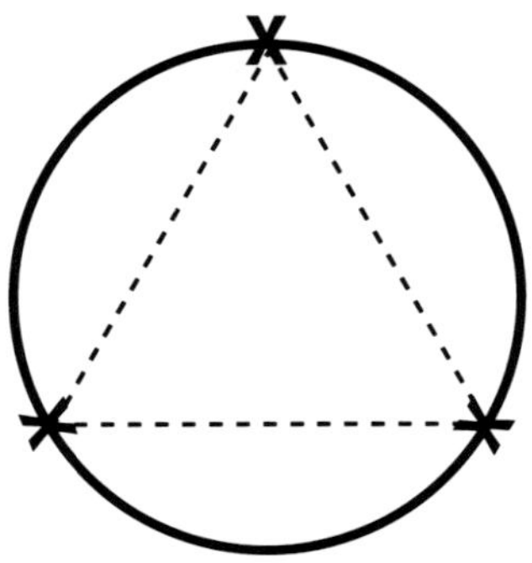

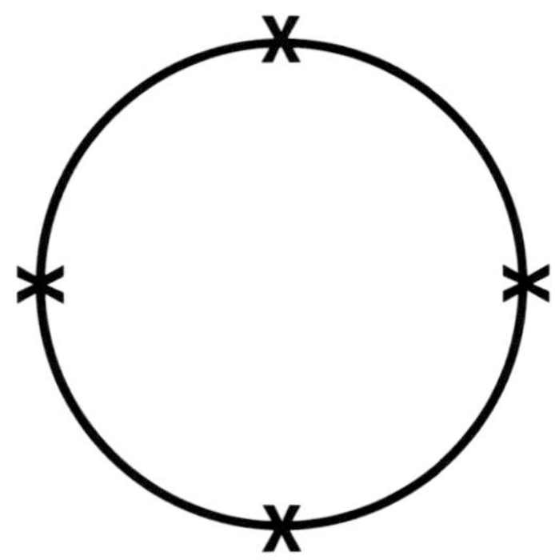

4 points need
_____ lines

5 points need
_____ lines

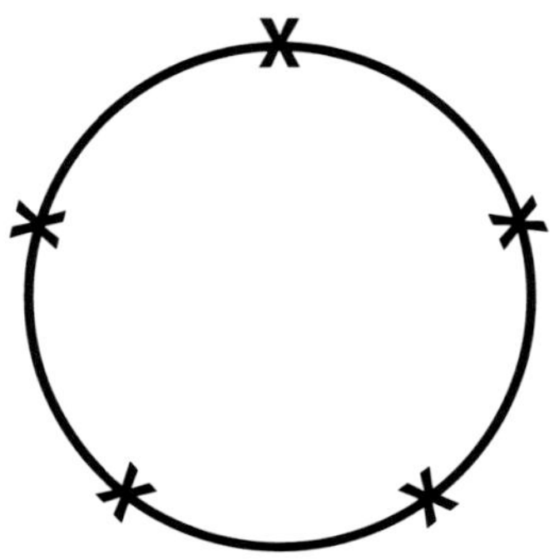

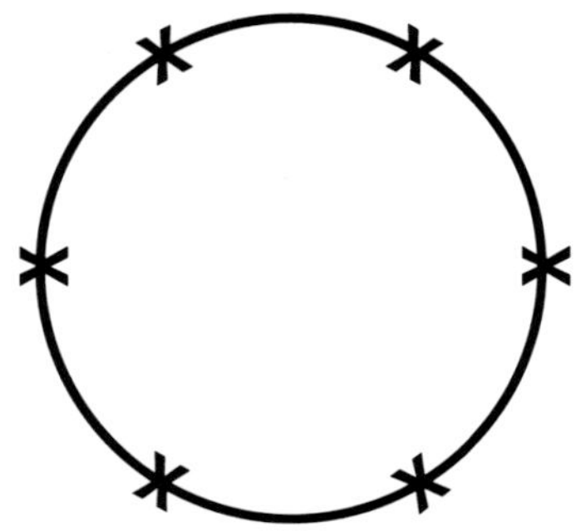

6 points need
_____ lines

7 points need
_____ lines

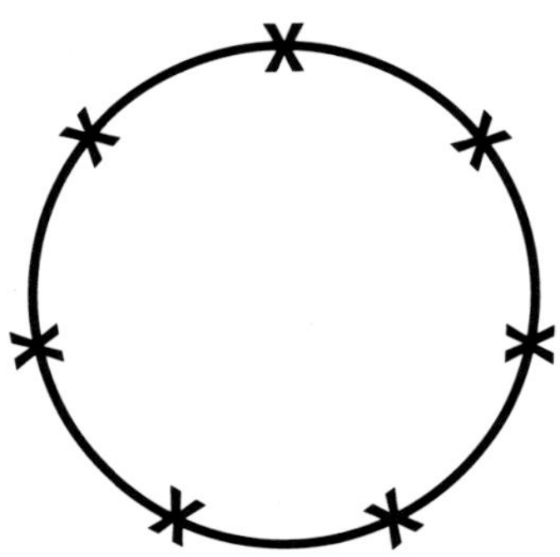

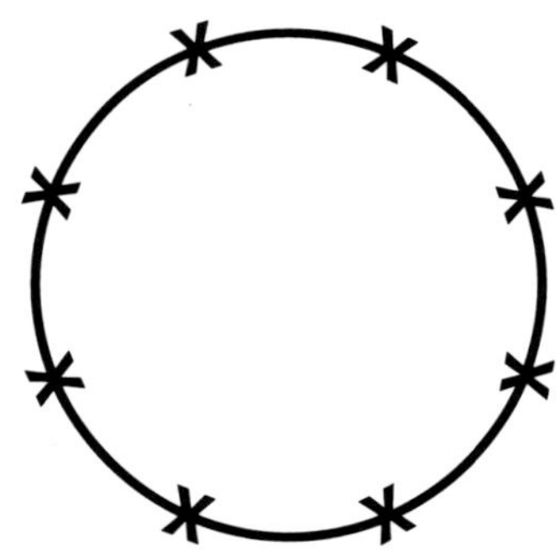

8 points need
_____ lines

Number of Points	3	4	5	6	7	8	9	10
Number of Lines								

Fill in the table above.
Find the rule to work out the number of lines needed to connect the points.
The rule is: ____

____

How many lines do you need to connect 9 and 10 points?

Completing Number Patterns

You often need to spot number patterns – both in the maths class and in life. Find the patterns and fill in the missing numbers below.

1.

1	2	3	4
5	6		8
	10		12
		15	

2.

2	4	6	8
10	12		16
		22	
		30	
			40
50			

3.

1	5	9	13
	21		29
		41	
	53		

4.

6	12		24		36			54			72	78				

5.

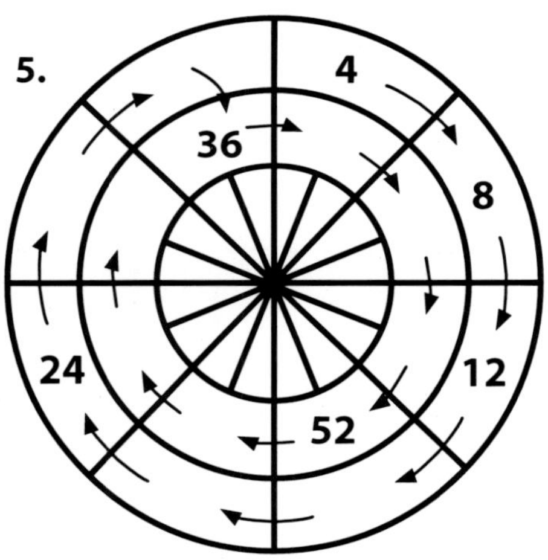

6.

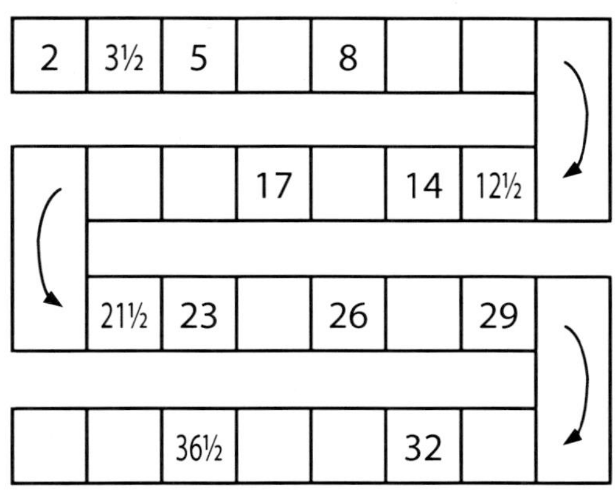

7.

1	2	4	7	11	16	22										

8.

2	6	18	54							

9.

66		62		58					48							34

Design your own number patterns below.

10.

11.

Following and Inventing Rules

Have a competition! Make a number follow the rules outside the boxes below and see if you all agree with the final number.

		÷2		+10		×3		−20		÷4
4	=	2	=	12	=	36	=	16	=	4
		÷3		×2		+25		÷9		×20
	=		=		=		=		=	
		×6		−12		÷2		×9		+19
	=		=		=		=		=	
		−4		×4		+74		÷10		÷9
	=		=		=		=		=	
		×4		×4		×4		×4		×4
	=		=		=		=		=	
		+5		×2		−2		×5		+20
	=		=		=		=		=	

Make up rules that start and end with the numbers below.
Have a +, -, x or ÷ rule for each square. Write the rules above the squares and the numbers they produce inside the squares as it is done above.

1	=		=		=		=		=	62
31	=		=		=		=		=	30
84	=		=		=		=		=	7

Working Out a Series from a Rule

Use the rules given below to work out the first 7 numbers in each series — let a=1, a=2, a=3, and so on. Also give the 10th, 27th and 40th numbers in the series. You can use a calculator!

RULE	1st term	2nd	3rd	4th	5th	6th	7th	10th	27th	40th
1. $a + 1$	**2**	**3**	**4**	**5**	**6**	**7**	**8**	**11**	**28**	**41**
2. $a + 9$										
3. $2a$										
4. $2a + 3$										
5. $a + a + a$										
6. $a/2$										
7. $10a$										
8. $3a - 2$										
9. $3a - a$										
10. $4(a + 1)$	**8**	**12**	**16**	**20**	**24**	**28**	**32**	**44**	**112**	**164**
11. $6(a - 1)$										
12. $5a + 4$										
13. $5(a + 4)$										
14. a^2										
15. $a^2 - a$										
16. $a + 2a + 3a$										
17. $a(a + 2)$										
18. $12a - 7$										
19. $a + \frac{1}{2}$										
20. $3a - a/2$										
21. $a^2 / 2$										
22. $1 - a$										
23. $5 - a$										
24. $1/a$										
25. a^3										
26. $\sqrt{a}$										
27. $20/a$										
28. $a(a-1)(a-2)$										

Working out Rules

All the boxes below perform an 'operation' on all the numbers coming in on the left hand side. Each number is changed and pushed out on the right hand side.

Inside each box, describe the operation performed by that box.

In	Rule Box 1	Out
1	Each number is	4
2	multiplied by 2	6
3	and 2 is added.	8
4		10
5		12
6		14

In	Rule Box 2	Out
1		4
2		7
3		10
4		13
5		16
6		19

In	Rule Box 3	Out
1		3
2		7
3		11
4		15
5		19
6		23

In	Rule Box 4	Out
1		1
2		4
3		9
4		16
5		25
6		36

In	Rule Box 5	Out
1		10
2		13
3		16
4		19
5		22
6		25

In	Rule Box 6	Out
1		1
2		6
3		11
4		16
5		21
6		26

In	Rule Box 7	Out
1	You invent	
2	a rule.	
3		
4		
5		
6		

In	Rule Box 8	Out
1	You invent	
2	a rule.	
3		
4		
5		
6		

Chase the Rule

There is space to play 3 games below. In a game, every player gets to throw one dice 24 times. Write each number you get in one of the 24 squares in the game. Once a number is written it cannot be changed. If the two numbers you write for a rule meet the conditions of the rule, you score one point. When you have filled in all 24 numbers for a game, add up the number of points that you score. The player who scores the most points is the winner.

Keep a tally on your number of throws.	1	2	3	4	5	6	7	8	9	10	11	12
	13	14	15	16	17	18	19	20	21	22	23	24

RULE FOR THE POINT	**Write the rule with 'variables' a and b**	**GAME 1**	**GAME 2**	**GAME 3**
Sum of 8	$a + b = 8$			
Difference of 3				
2nd double the 1st				
Both numbers odd				
Difference of 2	$a - b = 2$			
Sum greater than 10				
Both numbers even				
One is 3 x the other				
Sum is less than 4	$a + b < 4$			
Sum of 10				
Product of 12				
One half the other				
	Add up the score	**TOTAL**	**TOTAL**	**TOTAL**

Work Out Rules from Numbers

Look at the numbers in the columns marked A and B and see if you can find the rule to get from A to B. Write the rule underneath and complete the last two rows of B.

Clue: the difference between the numbers in successive rows of the B column is the number that the A values have to be multiplied by. ***But*** *also find out what else is done to the numbers.*

1.

A	B
1	6
2	8
3	10
4	12
5	14
16	**36**
20	**44**
B= A × 2 + 4	

2.

A	B
1	11
2	15
3	19
4	23
5	27
20	
50	
B=A ________	

3.

A	B
1	3
2	4
3	5
4	6
5	7
13	
24	
B=A ________	

4.

A	B
1	4
2	9
3	14
4	19
5	24
18	
25	
B=A ________	

5.

A	B
1	10
2	14
3	18
4	22
5	26
17	
32	
B=A ________	

6.

A	B
1	5
2	12
3	19
4	26
5	33
26	
28	
B=A ________	

7.

A	B
1	2
2	7
3	12
4	17
5	22
30	
50	
B=A ________	

8.

A	B
1	7
2	15
3	23
4	31
5	39
100	
200	
B=A ________	

9.

A	B
1	2½
2	3
3	3½
4	4
5	4½
11	
12	
B=A ________	

10.

A	B
1	0
2	11
3	22
4	33
5	44
9	
16	
B=A ________	

11.

A	B
1	3½
2	6½
3	9½
4	12½
5	15½
6	
16	
B=A ________	

12.

A	B
1	12
2	14
3	16
4	18
5	20
17	
54	
B=A ________	

Following Rules

Follow the rule written on the box to work out what number comes out of it.

1.

N	N + 2
1	3
2	4
3	5
4	6
10	12
20	22

2.

N	N + 7
1	
2	
3	
4	
10	
20	

3.

N	(N×2) + 1
1	
2	
3	
4	
10	
20	

4.

N	(N×4) – 1
1	
2	
3	
4	
10	
20	

5.

N	(N+6) × 2
1	
2	
3	
4	
10	
20	

6.

N	(N×10) – 5
1	
2	
3	
4	
10	
20	

7.

N	N × N
1	
2	
3	
4	
10	
20	

8.

N	(2xN) +20
1	
2	
3	
4	
10	
20	

9.

N	(3×N) +5
1	
2	
3	
4	
10	
20	

If the left hand side **(N)** represents the number of hours that you work and the right hand side represents the number of pounds you will earn, can you decide which rule is the best one to work out your pay if you work for 10 hours? What about if you work for 3 hours?

Grouping Similar Items

In the diagrams below, count up all the similar items as shown in the example.

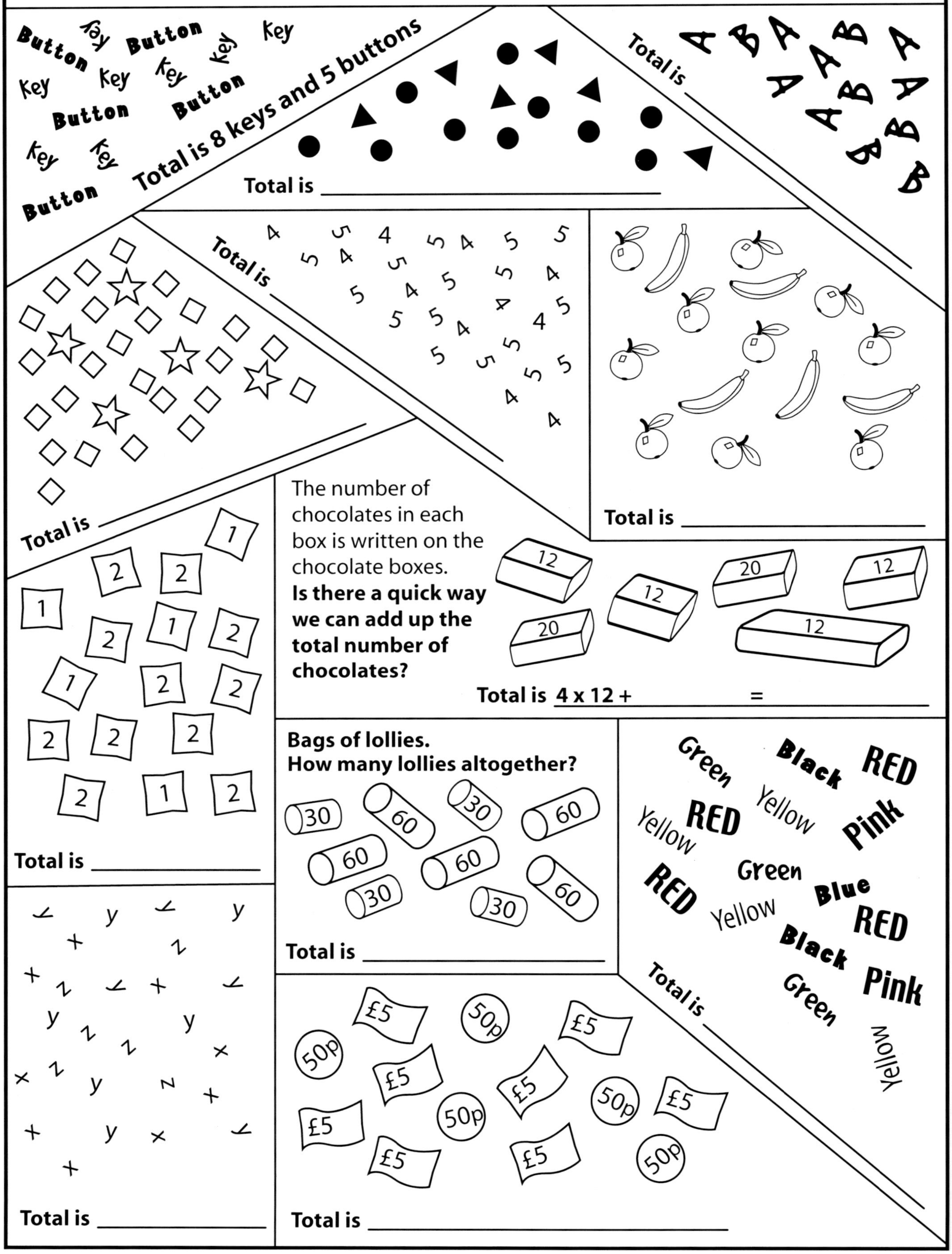

Sorting Collections into Groups

Use wooden or plastic cubes, counters and pencils to practise sorting groups of items into smaller groups that each contain the same number of each item.

Example

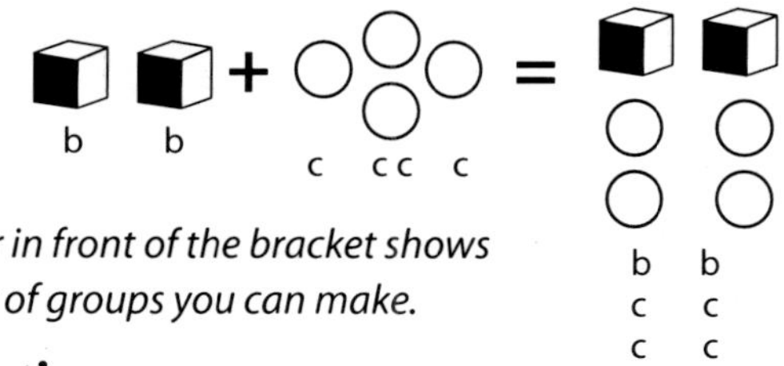

2b + 4c = 2(b + 2c)

b = blocks
c = counters

The number in front of the bracket shows the number of groups you can make.

Try the following collections:

1. 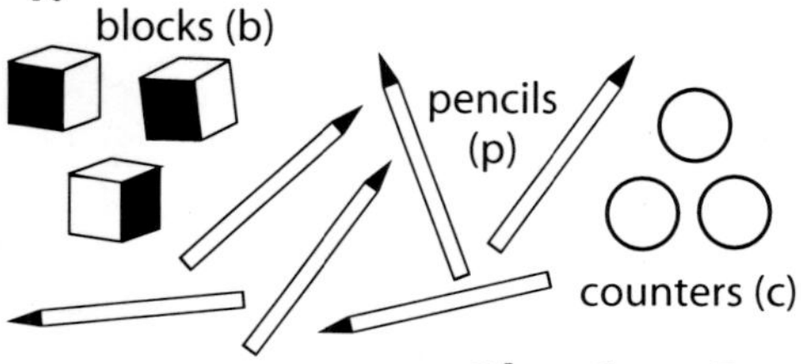 **3b + 6 p + 3c**	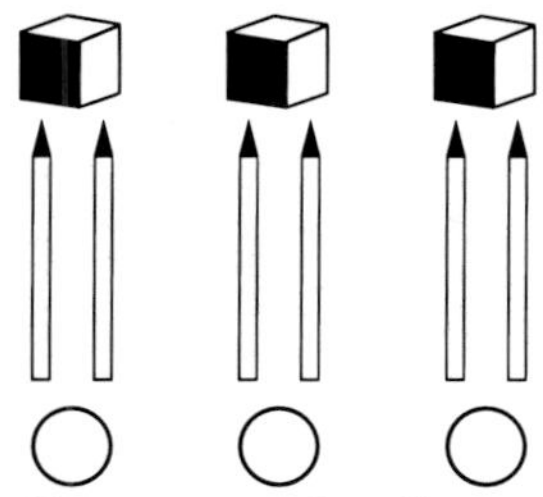 **= 3(b + 2p + c)** **(b + 2p + c) + (b + 2p + c) + (b + 2p + c)**
2. 6 p + 6c + 18b	______________________
3. 5c + 20b + 10p	______________________
4. 2p + 10c +8b	______________________
5. 7p + 14c + 21b	______________________
6. 4p + 2c + 6b	______________________
7. 3p + 3c + 9p + 3c Add similar items first.	______________________
8. 11p + 11c + 11 b	______________________
9. 5b + 5c + 3p *(Careful!)*	______________________
10. 2p + 2c + 12b	______________________

Collecting Similar Terms

info

Consider the following.

Multiplying:

8 x 2 = 2 x 8
3 x 6 = 6 x 3
20 x 5 = 5 x 20
So: a x b = b x a
And: ab = ba

Adding:

3 + 3 + 3 + 3 + 3 + 3 = 6 x 3
17 + 17 + 17 + 17 + 17 = 5 x 17
462 + 462 + 462 = 3 x 462
_ + _ + _ + _ + _ + _ = 6 x _
So: a + a + a + a = 4a

***Similar* or *like terms* can be collected together by adding or subtracting:**

3a + 7a + 4a + 6a	=	*20a*
17b – 11b	=	*6b*
xyz + 3xyz + 2xyz	=	*6xyz*
12xyz – 2xyz	=	*10xyz*
3ab + 2ba	=	*5ab*

Simplify the following.

1. 4a +5a + 6a + 1a = ______	**10.** 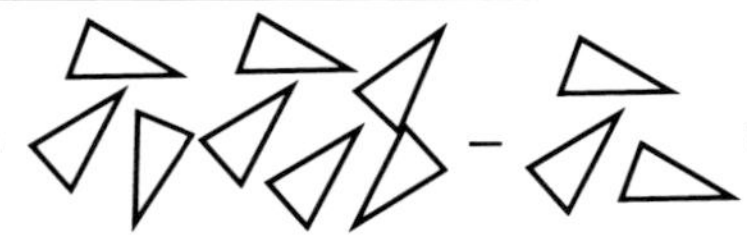 = 5 
2. 11c + 9c + 4c – 2c = ______	**11.** 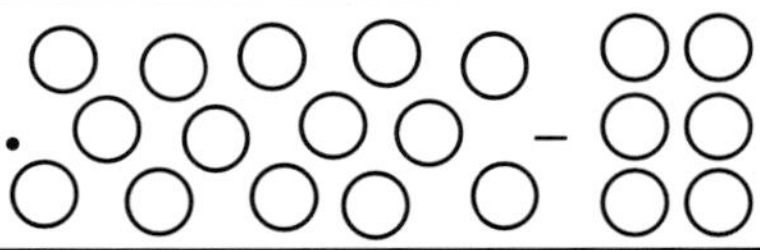 = 8 
3. d + d + d + d + d + 2d = ______	**12.**  = ______
4. ab + ba + 2ab + 7ab = ______	**13.**  = ______
5. 5y + 100y = ______	**14.** 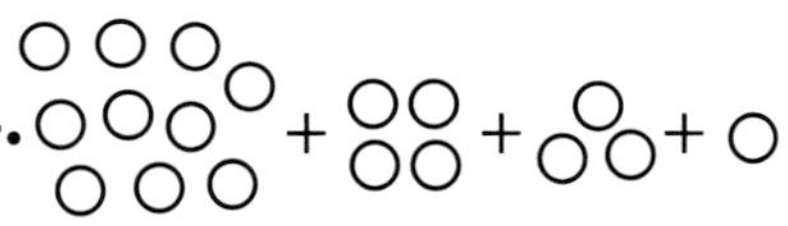 = ______
6. 12r – r – r = ______	**15.** c + 2c + 3c + 4c + 5c + 6c = ______
7. 35cd – 4cd = ______	**16.** 13ab + 5ba + 7ab +2ab = ______
8. 30a + 40a + 60a – 50a = ______	**17.** 428y + 20y – 15y = ______
9. 15f + 3f + 7f – 25f = ______	**18.** 12b + 3b + 401b = ______

Collecting Like Terms

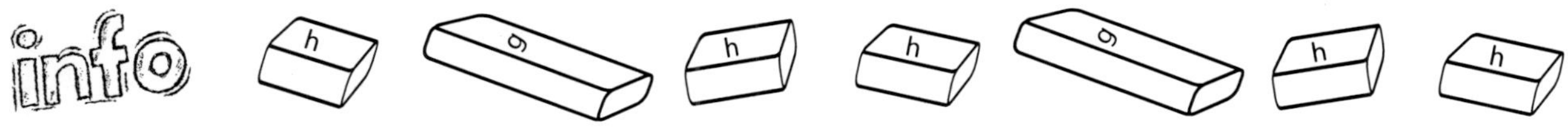

The large boxes above each contain **'g'** number of chocolates and the smaller boxes each contain **'h'** number of chocolates. To work out the total number of chocolates we have to collect all the 'similar' or 'like' boxes.

Our boxes could be written as	h + g + h + h + g + h + h
When we collect terms we get	= 2 x g + 5 x h
which we write as	**= 2g + 5h**

Collect the like terms in each question below.

1. a + a + a + b + a + b = **4a + 2b**	**11.** 6e + e + e + 4f + f + 3f = ______
2. 3x + 3y + 7x + 10y + x = ______	**12.** 4x + 2x – x + 10y – 6y = ______
3. 10c + 3a + 10a + 21c + c = ______	**13.** g + 2g + 4g – g + 11h – 3h = ______
4. 4a + 2a + 3a = ______	**14.** 6a + 8a + 2b = ______
5. 3a + 6a + 7b + 6b + c = ______	**15.** 100x + 100y + 100z = ______
6. 30w + 11x + 3x + y + 6y = ______	**16.** 30x – 3x + 15y – 6y = ______
7. 15a + 15b + c + d = ______	**17.** 200x – 17x + 3z + y = ______
8. 22x - 5x + 3y – 7 = ______	**18.** 17j + 7j + j + 3xy + xy = ______
9. 6p + e + 20f – 6p = ______	**19.** 14j – 6j + 3k – 3k – 8j = ______
10. a + b + c + d + 4a + 3c + 12d + 2d + 3b = ______	**20.** 12b + 30b + 6 + c + d – 42b + d - 2d + 2d = ______

Writing Rules

Write a "general" expression for the following operations. The letter M represents any number.

1. Twice the number	**2 x M**
2. Half the number	
3. The next consecutive number	
4. Four times that number	
5. The square of the number	
6. The square root of the number	
7. Multiply the number by 2 and add 6.	**M x 2 + 6**
8. The difference between the number and 10.	
9. One fifth of the number.	
10. What distance is the race?	

Give an expression for the sum of the following quantities.

11. M + M + M + M + M	**5 x M**
12. 6 + 8 + M	
13. A + B + B + B	
14. x + y + 3	
15. 28 + M + M	
16. B + B + B +B + B + B	

Give an expression for the difference between the following two quantities.
(The number on the left is the largest)

17. 20 and 17	**20 – 17**
18. M and N	
19. 31 and x	
20. 100 and y	
21. P and Q	

Find a different way to write the following.

22. 5 + 5 + 5 + 5 + 7	**4 x 5 + 7**
23. a + a + a + a + a + a + a + b	
24. 3 x a	
25. x + x + x + x + y + y + y + y + y	

Calendar Problems

Sunday	Monday	Tuesday	Wednesday	Thursday	Friday	Saturday

Add numbers to the above calendar so that it applies to the current month.
Look for patterns in the following way.

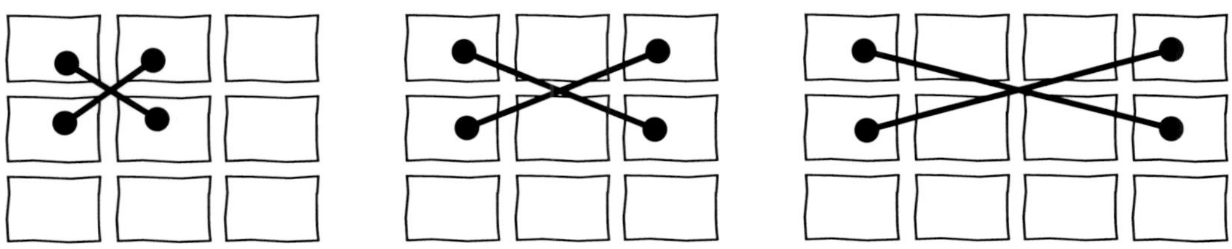

What do you notice when you add the diagonals in the above cases?

____

info

8	9
15	16

Pick on any four numbers that form a square on the calendar.
Notice that 9 x 15 – 8 x 16 = 7

Prove that b x c – a x d will always be 7. (Hard!)

a	b
c	d

____

____

____

____

____

Working Out Perimeters

Work out a way to find the perimeter of each shape below and write this down using the letters. Then, use the actual numbers given for the letters to find the actual distance around the object.

1.

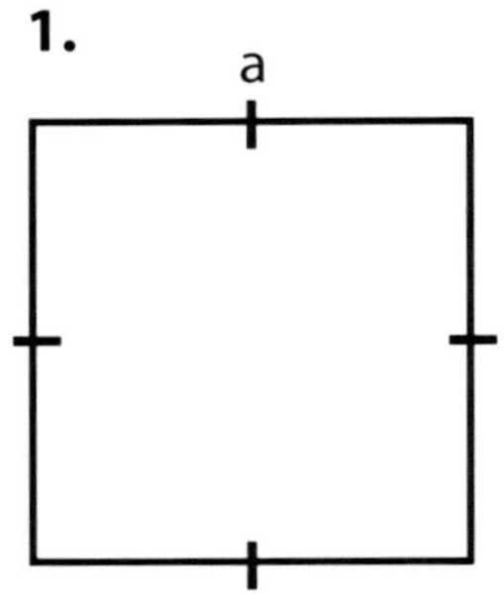

Perimeter (P) = **a + a + a + a**

If a = 2 cm

P = **2 + 2 + 2 + 2 = 8 cm**

If a = 7 km

P = **7 + 7 + 7 + 7 = 28 km**

2.

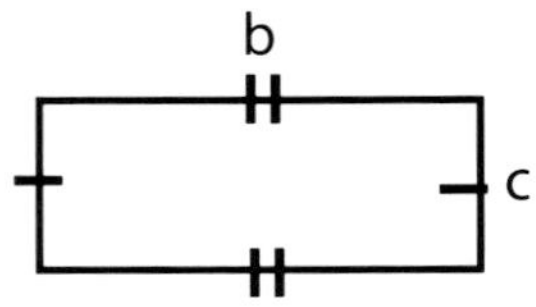

P = ____________

If b = 6 cm; c = 3 cm

P = ____________

If b = 10 m; c = 2 m

P = ____________

3.

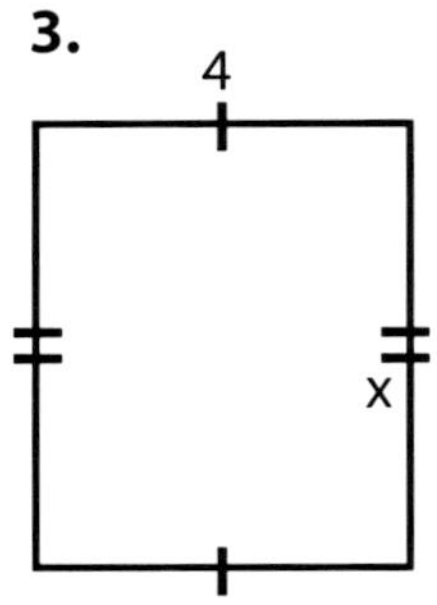

P = ____________

If x = 31 m

P = ____________

If x = 15 km

P = ____________

4.

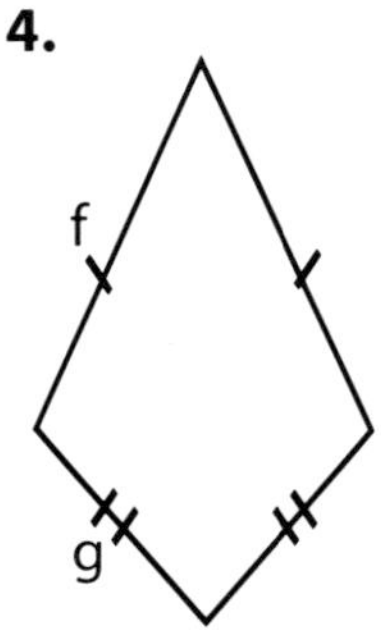

P = ____________

If f = 14 cm; g = 7 cm

P = ____________

If f = 20 cm; g = 16 cm

P = ____________

5.

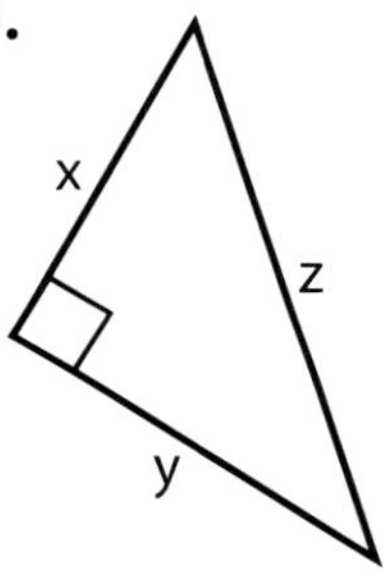

P = ____________

If x = 3cm; y = 4 cm; z = 5 cm

P = ____________

If x = 5 cm; y = 12 cm; z = 13 cm

P = ____________

6.

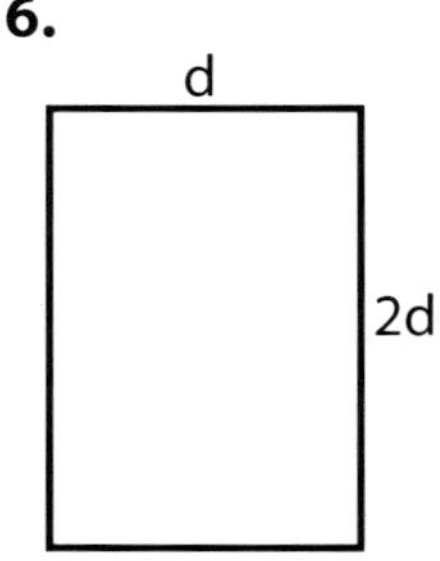

P = ____________

If d = 7 km

P = ____________

If d = 0.5 cm

P = ____________

7.

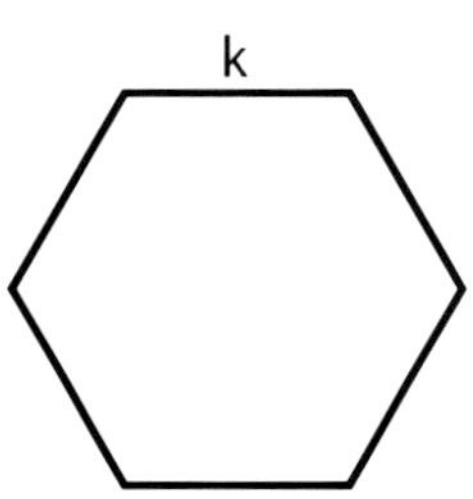

P = ____________

If k = 3 cm

P = ____________

If k = 1.6 m

P = ____________

8.

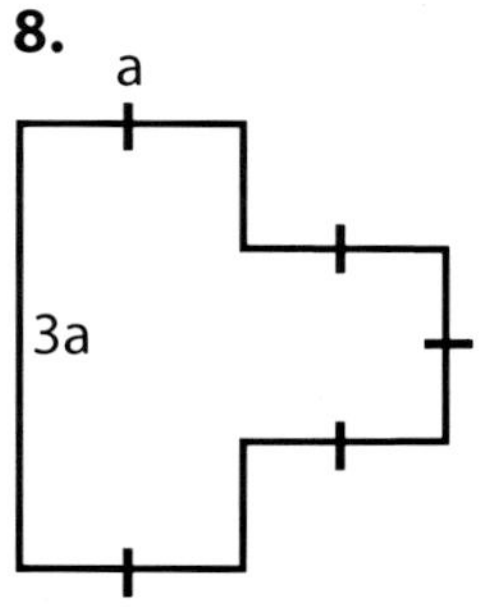

P = ____________

If a = 5 cm

P = ____________

If a = 22 m

P ____________

9.

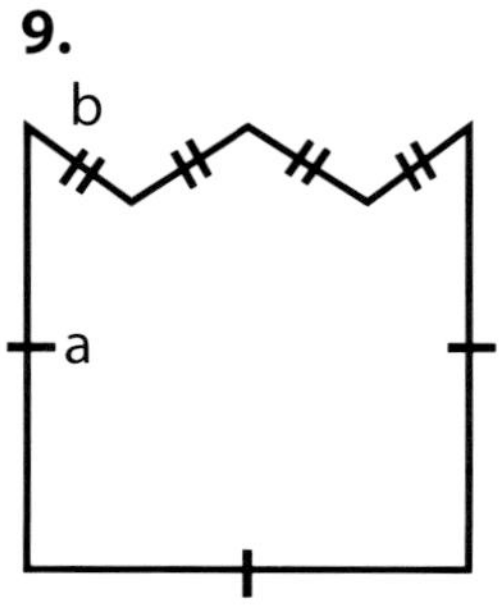

P = ____________

If a = 9 cm; b = 2 cm

P = ____________

If a = 18 cm; b = 4 cm

P = ____________

10.

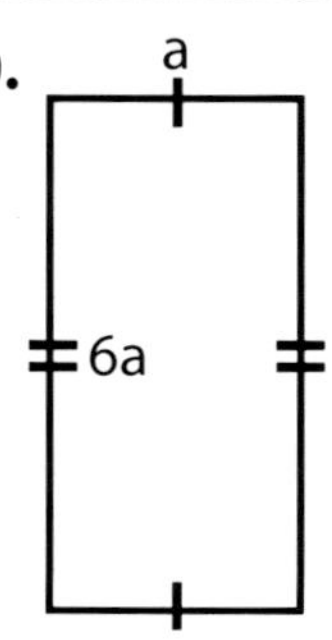

P = ____________

If a = 22 cm

P = ____________

If a = 0.5 m

P = ____________

If a = 16 m

P = ____________

Solving Problems with Equations

Write an algebraic expression for the following statements and then find the solution. The first one has been done for you.

1. When 3 is added to this number the total is 14

a + 3 = 14 so a = 14 – 3 = 11

2. When I take 22 from the number I get 17

3. When we double this number and take away 7 we get 29

4. A quarter of this number is 44

5. The square of this number plus the number is 42

6. If you add 4 to this number and multiply the result by 9 you get 81

7. If you double this number and double it again you finish up with 72

8. The perimeter of this shape is 135 m long and consists of 5 equal sides, so how long is each side?

9. If we double this number and then multiply it by 7 we get 70

10. A school of 16 classes has a total of 464 students. How large are the classes?

Each line is 3 cm longer that the previous line. The total length is 385 cm. How long was the first line?

Substituting Numbers and Letters

Use grouping symbols to write expressions for the following.

info *Example: Add 20 to the difference between 7 and 3* → ***(7-3) + 20***

1. Take 50 from the total of 17, 12 and 100
2. Add 10 to the square of 11
3. Divide 62 by 31 and add 9
4. To the product of 6 and 2, add 3
5. To the product of a and b, add c
6. Multiply 3 by 10 and take away 4
7. Multiply a by b and take away c
8. Take 20 from the difference between x and y

Find the numerical value of the following.
Let a = 8, b = 6, c = 4, d = 3

1. $a + b =$	**2.** $a \times b =$	**3.** $a + b + c + d =$	**4.** $a + b - c =$
5. $c^2 =$	**6.** $3bd =$	**7.** $(a + b + c) \div d =$	**8.** $(a - b) \times (c + d) =$
9. $4a - bc =$	**10.** $b \times c \div d =$	**11.** $a^2 - d^2 =$	**12.** $3a - c^2 =$
13. $a + a + b + b + b =$	**14.** $(cd)^2 =$	**15.** $3c + d =$	**16.** $4a - 4b =$
17. $(a + b) \times 6 =$	**18.** $b \times b \times b =$	**19.** $c^3 =$	**20.** $abcd =$

Finding Variables in a Rectangle

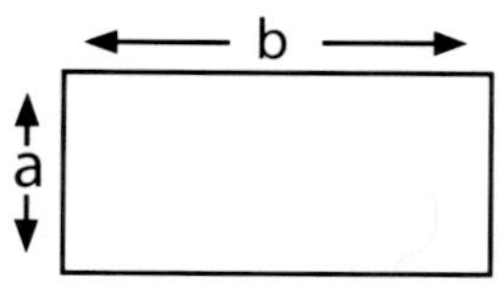

Imagine each square below has a side of 1 cm. Draw as many rectangles as you can of different sizes, but all with a perimeter of 36 cm. One side is represented by 'a' and the other by 'b'. Fill in the data sheet and see if you can see a link between a, b and the area of the rectangle (A).
To find the area, count the squares inside the rectangle. So the variables in the rectangle are -__ , __ and __. Perimeter (P) is a constant.

a	b	P	A

The Magic Square

info *In a magic square, all the numbers on the horizontal, vertical and diagonal lines add up to the same total. We can make such a square using three variables –* ***a****,* ***b****, and* ***c****. Look at the way the letters a, b and c are organised in the square below.*

Work out that all lines do add up to the same total. Two lines have been done for you.

a – b	a + b – c	a + c	=
a + b + c	a	a – b – c	=
a – c	a – b + c	a + b	**a+a+a–b+b–c+c = 3a**

Diagonal: **a+a+a–c+c = 3a**

Other diagonal: =

Columns: = = =

Use the values of a, b and c below to fill in the numbers in the squares.
(You will have some negative numbers.)

a = 10 b = 8 c = 4

a = 9 b = 6 c = 1

a = 5 b = 3 c = 4

Graphing the Plumber

A plumber charges for house calls at the following rate:

c = 16h + 8

where c = charge in pounds and h = the number of hours worked

Work out a table of charges for working up to 8 hours.

Number of hours worked	Calculation	Charge (c) (£)
1		
2		
3		
4		
5		
6		
7		
8		

Plot a graph below of the amount charged compared to the number of hours worked.

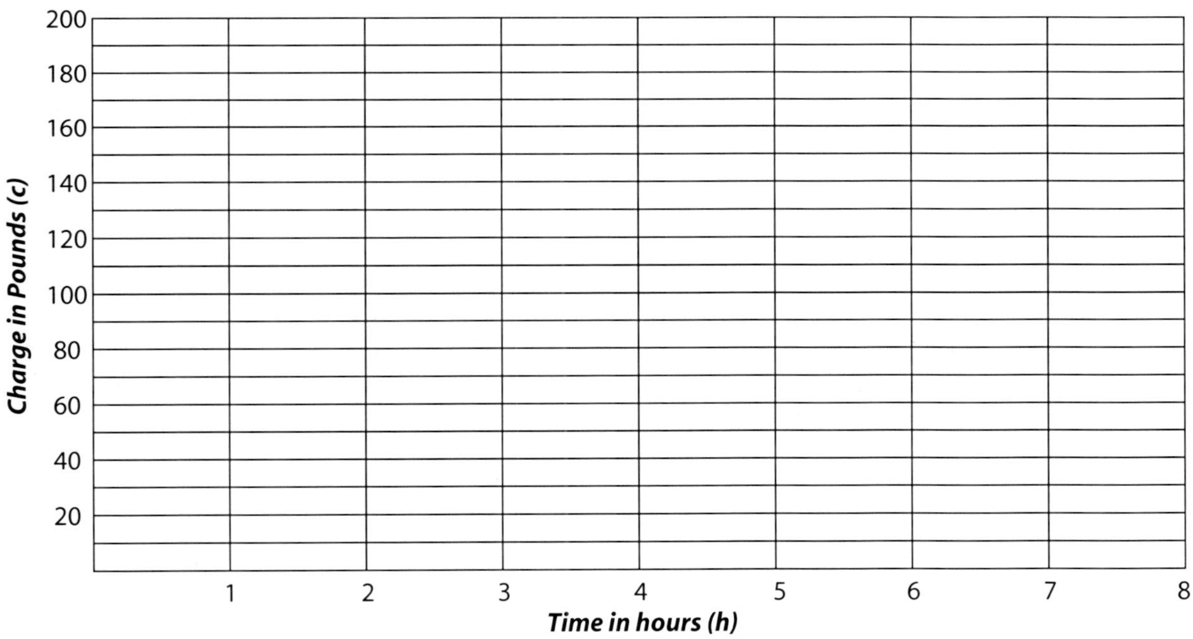

Answer the following questions.

1. How much does the plumber charge for 4 ½ hours work? ____________
2. If the plumber charged £112 how long was the work period? ____________
3. How much is charged if 40 hours are worked? *(Use the fact that c = 16h + 8)* ____________

Odds and Evens

Let **E** stand for any even number and **O** stand for any odd number.

Cut out the E's and O's and the x, –, +, – and = signs below. Then make up your own equations. For more challenging problems include the numbers 1 to 9 in the equations.

Examples:

$E + 1 = O$

$E \times 2 = E$

$E + 5 + E = O$

$O + E + O + E + O = O$

Try:

$E + O =$ ____________

$E + E =$ ____________

$O \times 2 =$ ____________

$4 \times E =$ ____________

E	E	E	E	E	E	E	E	E	E
O	O	O	O	O	O	O	O	O	O
X	X	X	X	÷	÷	÷	÷	+	+
+	+	–	–	+	+	=	=	=	=
10	20	30	40	1	2	3	4	5	6
7	8	9	1	2	3	4	5	6	7
8	9	1	2	3	4	5	6	7	8
9	1	2	3	4	5	6	7	8	9

Set problems for other people and ask them to find if the answer is an odd number or an even number.

Spotting Patterns 1

Use counters or pieces of paper to find triangular and square numbers.

Square numbers

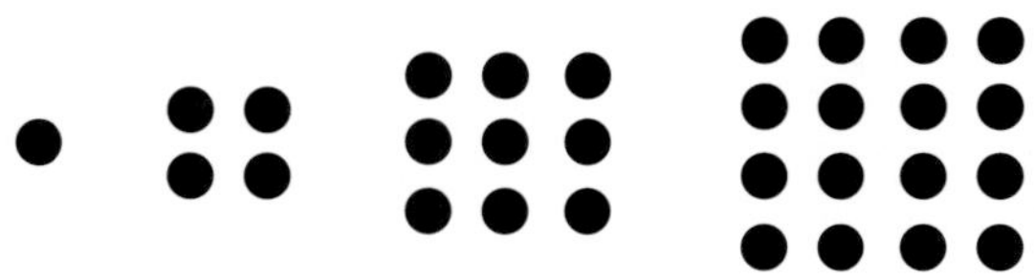

Find 4 more square numbers

______ ______ ______ ______

Triangular numbers

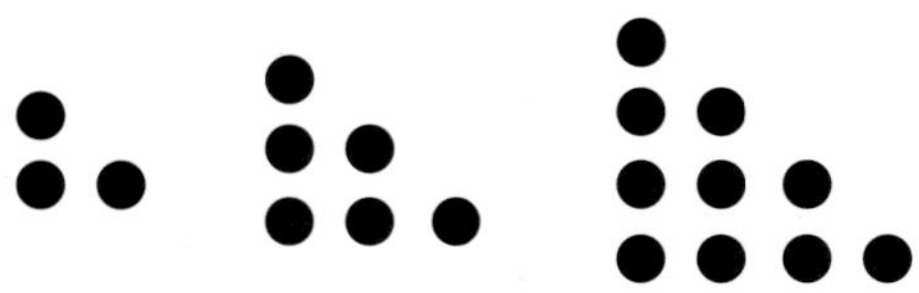

Find 4 more triangular numbers

______ ______ ______ ______

Spotting Patterns 2

Find the next 4 numbers in the series below.

1	2	3	4	___	___	___	___
2	4	6	8	___	___	___	___
1	5	9	13	___	___	___	___
3	6	9	12	___	___	___	___
1	2	4	7	___	___	___	___
10	14	18	22	___	___	___	___
30	28	26	24	___	___	___	___
0	7	14	21	___	___	___	___
40	35	30	25	___	___	___	___
1	2	4	8	___	___	___	___
20	17	14	11	___	___	___	___
60	52	44	36	___	___	___	___

Making Patterns

Make up your own number patterns.

1. Keep multiplying the number by 2

1 **2** **4** **8** **16** **32** **64** **128**

2. Add 11 to the previous number

0 ___ ___ ___ ___ ___ ___ ___

3. Multiply by 2 and add 1

1 ___ ___ ___ ___ ___ ___ ___

4. Start with 5 and keep adding 9

5 ___ ___ ___ ___ ___ ___ ___

5. Start with 100 and take 13 off each number

100 ___ ___ ___ ___ ___ ___ ___

6. Start with 800 and keep dividing by 2

800 ___ ___ ___ ___ ___ ___ ___

7. Start with 0 and keep adding your age

0 ___ ___ ___ ___ ___ ___ ___

Spot the Rule

The boxes below carry out an operation on the number going into them. Discover this operation and find the missing numbers coming out.

IN	OUT
1	2
2	4
3	6
4	8
5	
6	

IN	OUT
1	4
2	7
3	10
4	
5	16
6	

IN	OUT
1	3
2	7
3	11
4	
5	
6	23

IN	OUT
1	7
2	12
3	17
4	22
5	
6	

Rule Boxes

The boxes below carry out an operation on the number going into them. Discover this operation and find the missing numbers coming out.

IN	OUT
1	½
2	1
3	1½
4	
5	
6	

IN	OUT
1	1½
2	2
3	2½
4	
5	3½
10	

IN	OUT
1	8
2	13
3	18
4	23
5	
10	

IN	OUT
1	2
2	9
3	16
4	
5	
8	51

Building Patterns 1

Use matchsticks to build up the pattern below. Extend this pattern up to 6 squares and fill in the table.

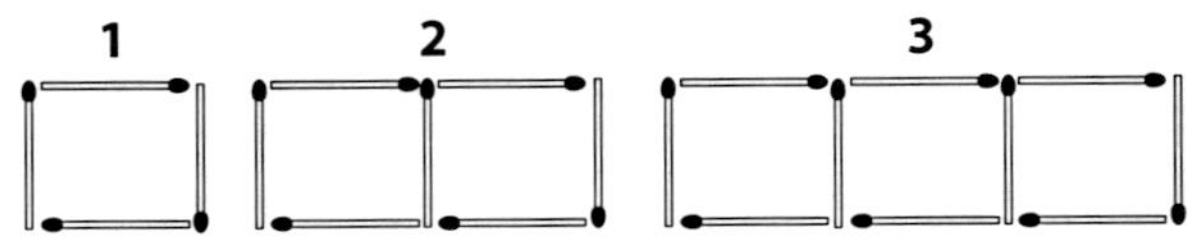

Is there a rule to decide match numbers for any number of squares?

Number of squares	1	2	3	4	5	6
Number of sticks	4	7	10			
Rule						

How many matches would be needed to make 100 squares? ____________________
(Use the rule to work this out).

Building Patterns 2

Use matchsticks to build up the pattern below. Extend the patterns up to 6 side lengths and fill in the table below.

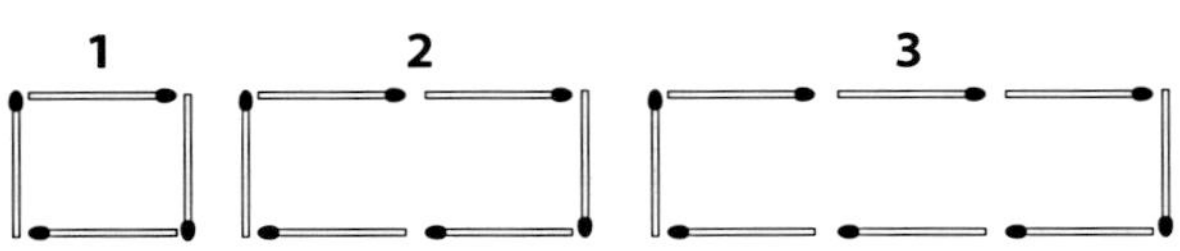

Is there a rule you can use to work out matches needed to make a particular side length?

Length of side	1	2	3	4	5	6
Number of sticks						
Rule						

For 10 side lengths _____ matches are needed
For 30 side lengths _____ matches are needed
For 100 side lengths _____ matches are needed

Building Patterns 3

Use matchsticks to build up the pattern below. Extend the patterns up to 6 side lengths and fill in the table below.

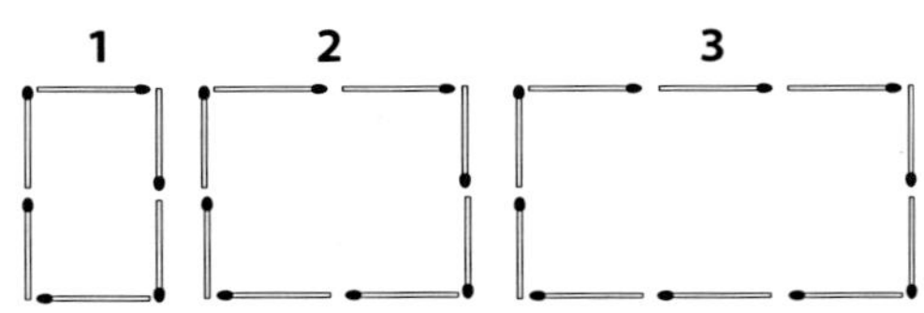

Is there a rule you can use to work out matches needed to make a particular side length?

Length of side	1	2	3	4	5	6
Number of sticks						
Rule						

For 20 side lengths _____ matches are needed
For 45 side lengths _____ matches are needed
For 100 side lengths _____ matches are needed

Using Rules 1

General expressions provide us with a way of saying what operation we are performing on a set of numbers.

Example
General Expression **(n + 4)**
when n is 1, 2, 3, 4, etc.

N	N + 4
1	5
2	6
3	7
4	8

Try the expression (2n + 1)

N	2N + 1
1	**3**
2	
3	
4	

Using Rules 2

General expressions. Fill in the tables below.

N	N + 2
1	
2	
3	
4	
5	

N	2 N
1	
2	
3	
4	
10	

N	3N + 1
1	
2	
3	
4	
10	

N	3N – 1
1	
2	
3	
4	
10	

Using Rules 3

General expressions. Fill in the tables below.

N	5N + 2
1	
2	
3	
4	
10	

N	N^2
1	
2	
3	
4	
10	

N	4N
1	
2	
3	
4	
8	

N	6N – 5
1	
2	
3	
4	
7	

Using Rules 4

General expressions. Fill in the tables below.

N	2N + 10
1	
2	
3	
4	
20	

N	$N^2 - 1$
1	
2	
3	
4	
10	

N	$N^2 - N$
1	
2	
3	
4	
10	

You invent a rule!

N	
1	
2	
3	
4	
10	

More Sequences

Find the first 6 terms and the 10th term of the following expressions.

	n=1	n=2	n=3	n=4	n=5	n=6	n=10
n + 4	**5**	**6**	**7**	**8**	**9**	**10**	**11**
2 x n	**2**	**4**	**6**	**8**	**10**	**12**	**20**
3n							
2n + 1							
2n – 1							
n^2							
4n							
2n + 5							
10n							
10n – 10							
$\frac{n}{2}$							

Perimeters 1

Find expressions for the perimeters of the shapes below.

1.
P = ______________

If a = 3, b = 5
Perimeter is ________
If a = 7, b = 10
Perimeter is ________

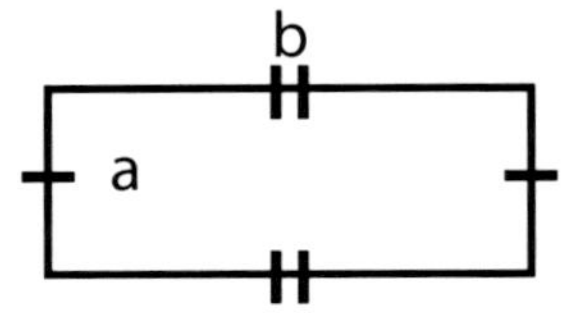

2.
P = ______________

If a = 11
Perimeter is ________
If a = 8
Perimeter is ________

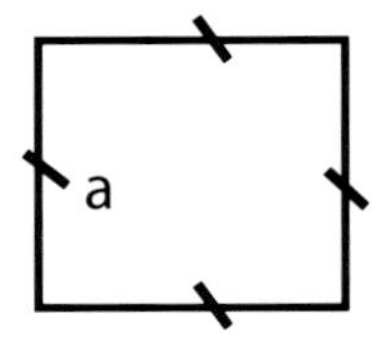

3.
P = ______________

If a = 3
Perimeter is ________

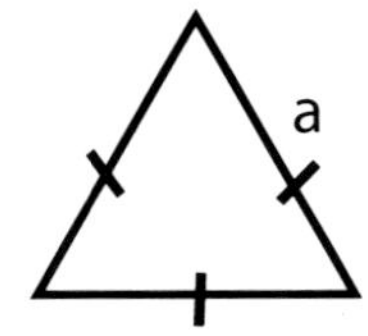

Perimeters 2

Find expressions for the perimeters (P) of the shapes below.

1.
P = ______________

____

If a = 2, b = 6
P = ____________
If a = 7, b = 21
P = ____________

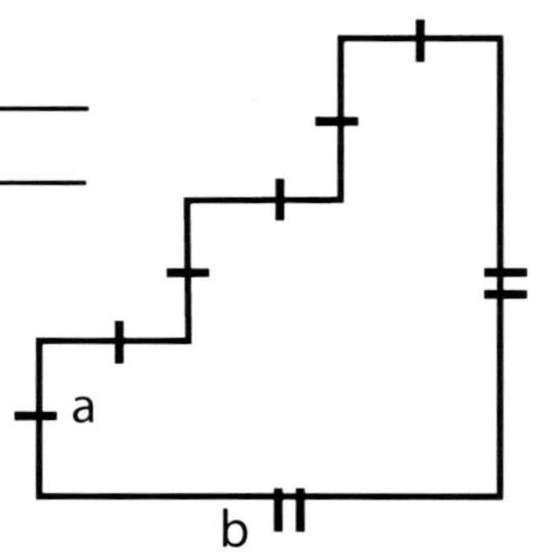

2.
P = ______________

If a = 2, b = 4, c = 6
P = ____________
If a = 6, b = 10, c = 16
P = ____________

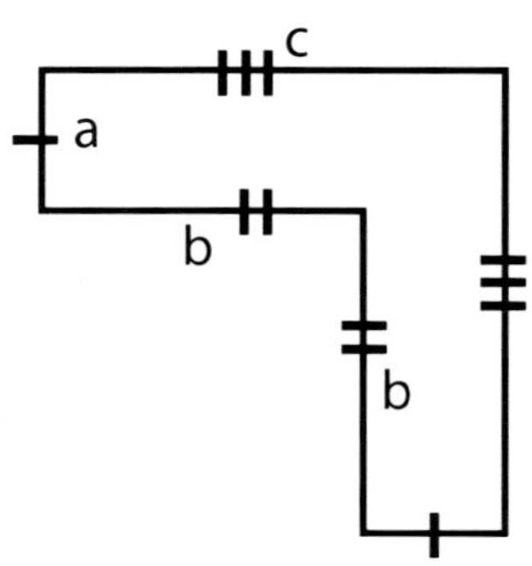

Perimeters 3

Find a number of values for the variables x and y if the perimeter is always 30 cm.

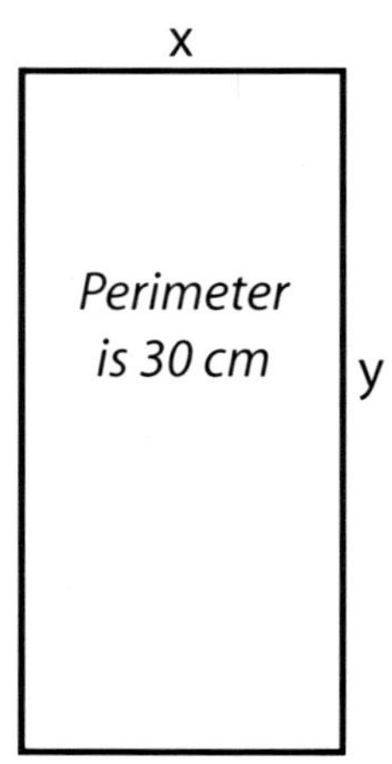

x	y

x	y

Rectangle Variables

A rectangle has a perimeter of 40 m. The length and breadth can vary but the perimeter must stay 40 m.

Can you think of some lengths and widths?

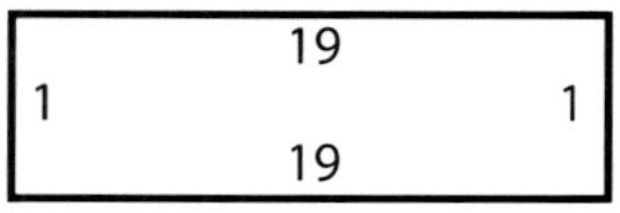

Length	Width	Length	Width
19	**1**		
18			

Algebra Rules

Let 'a' represent any number. Find an expression for each of the following.

1. 5 times the number **5a or 5 x a**
2. That number plus 4 ______
3. That number squared ______
4. The square root of the number ______
5. 3 times the number plus 1 ______
6. That number from 100 ______
7. Half that number ______
8. That number less 2 ______
9. That number multiplied by the next consecutive number ______
10. A quarter of that number ______

Rewriting Rules

Can you write these expressions in a different way?

1. a + a + a + a = **4 x a**
2. y + y + y + y = ______
3. 3 x a = ______
4. a + b + a + b + a + b + a = ______
5. d + e + f + e + e + d = ______
6. 3 x a + 2b = ______
7. w + z + y + y = ______
8. n + m + n + m + 4 = ______
9. 4 x b = ______
10. 4 x b – 7 = ______
11. 4 x b -7 + b = ______
12. 6f = ______
13. 2f + 3q = ______

More Expressions

Write an expression for these.

1. Add 4 to the product of 3 and 6
   4 + (3 x 6)
2. Take 20 from the square of 12
   ______
3. Multiply the sum of 15 and 21 by 16
   ______
4. Take 11 from the product of a and b
   ______
5. Divide 6 by a and add 7
   ______
6. Multiply a and b and c together
   ______
7. The difference between 28 and d
   ______

Larger Triangle

The triangle has sides of 5, 7 and 10 cm. If you increase side 1 by x cm, side 2 by y cm and side 3 by z cm, what would the perimeter of the new triangle be?

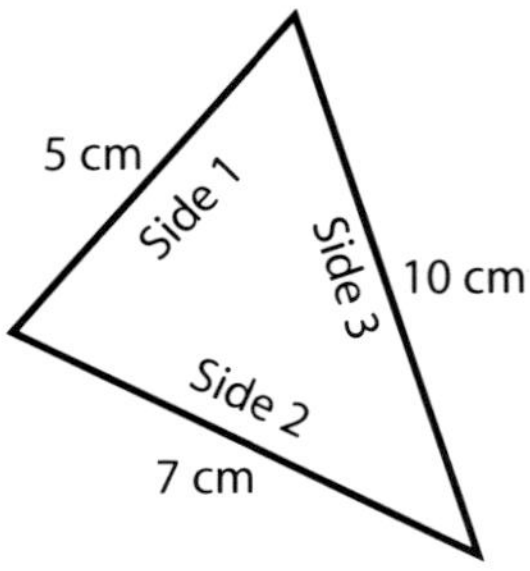

Draw the new triangle and write the expression for its perimeter below.

____

____

____

Perimeter and Area

Write down the perimeter of this rectangle.

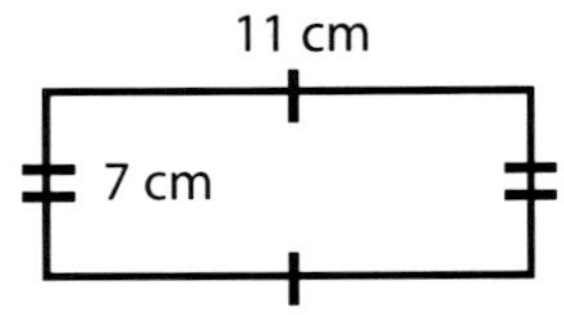

____

Increase the 11 cm side by 'a' cm and the 7 cm side by 'b' cm.

Write an expression for the new perimeter. ____________________

____

____

Write an expression for the area of the new triangle.

____

____

Collecting Terms

Collect the like terms below.

1. a + a + a + a + 1 = __________

2. x + 2x + 7x + x = __________

3. a + 2b + 5a + b + c = __________

4. w + w + w + w + y = __________

5. 2x + 10x + y + 4y = __________

6. 4y + z + 11y + 3y = __________

7. 12x – x - 4x + 4 = __________

8. a + 2b + c + 8a + 7c = __________

9. 46b + 18c – 17a + 6 = __________

10. 17x – 5x + 7y + 10y = __________

11. 11m – 2m + 18n – 9n = __________

12. 7x + 9y – 7y – 3y = __________

13. 20b – 8b – 8b – 4b = __________

14. 246y – 23x + 10y = __________

Ungrouping

info

The area of the card here can be written as

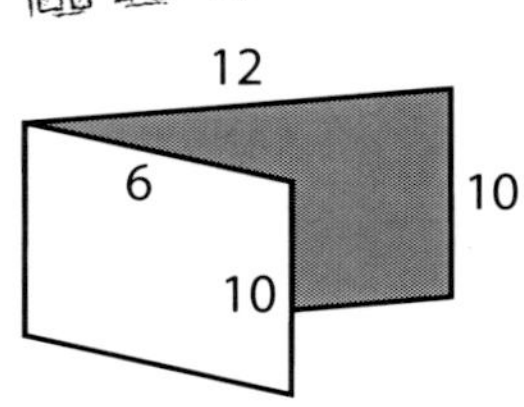

10(6 + 12)
= 10 x 6 + 10 x 12
= 60 + 120
= 180 cm²

Remove the grouping symbols below.

1. 9(8 + 6) = __________

2. 3(a + b) = __________

3. 4(x + 8) = __________

4. a(b + c) = __________

5. 7(3x + 5) = __________

6. 10(b + b) = __________

Easier Expressions

One way to remove brackets that group things is shown below.

2(x + 2y) means
(x + 2y) + (x + 2y)
= x + 2 y + x + 2y
= 2x + 4y

An easier way is to multiply everything in the bracket by the number or letter outside the bracket, as follows.

2(x + 2y) = 2x + 4y

Simplify the following.

7(3x + 2y) = ____________

3(5 + 4x) = ____________

Removing Brackets

Remove the brackets and collect like terms.

1. 6(2x + y + z) = **12x + 6y + 6z**
2. 5(10a + 3b) = ____________
3. 10(2d + x + 5k) = ____________
4. ½(4a + 6b) = ____________
5. 7(4x + 6y) = ____________
6. a(b + c) = ____________
7. 4z(2y + x) = ____________
8. 3(a + b) + 4(a + c) = ____________
9. 4x + 3(5x + 2y) = ____________
10. 3(2t + 3) + 11(4t + 1) = ____________
11. 6(a + b + c) + 11b = ____________

Sorting Expressions

Simplify these expressions by including brackets.

1. 2a + 2b = **2(a + b)**
2. 6x + 12y + 18 = **6(x + 2y + 3)**
3. 2a + 2b + 2c = ____________
4. 3x + 6y = ____________
5. 5c + 15d + 10e = ____________
6. 7a + 28 = ____________
7. 12 + 6a = ____________
8. ab + 6a = ____________
9. 5g + g = ____________
10. 60a + 120ac = ____________
11. 4ab + 2ab = ____________
12. ad + d = ____________
13. 3p + 6m + 18n = ____________

Solving Equations

Solve the following equations by finding the number x.

1. x + 2 = 6 **x = 6 - 2 = 4**
2. x – 8 = 10 ____________
3. x ÷ 3 = 4 ____________
4. $x^2 = 16$ ____________
5. 3x = 9 ____________
6. 2x + 1 = 5 ____________
7. 2x + 1 = 7 ____________
8. 2x +1 = 9 ____________
9. $\sqrt{x} = 4$ ____________
10. x + 8 = 24 ____________
11. $x^2 + 1 = 26$ ____________
12. x ÷ 5 = 6 ____________
13. $x^2 = 49$ ____________
14. 6x = 60 ____________

Toss a Coin

info
- ***Statistics*** *involves collecting and displaying data.*
- ***Predictions*** *involve the analysis of data resulting in educated guesses as to what will happen in future or under different circumstances.*
- *When we try to predict the chance of something happening we are dealing with* ***probability****.*

If you toss a coin 40 times, what is the predicted tally of heads and tails?
Try it out and record your results below.

Outcome	Tally	Total
Head		
Tail		

Do your results fit your prediction? Exactly? Approximately? ____________________

____

Toss 2 Coins

Toss two coins 40 times and record the results below. You can tick numbers 1 to 40 to keep count.
Note: you can observe a HH, HT, or TH outcome (H is heads, T is tails).

1	2	3	4	5	6	7	8	9	10
11	12	13	14	15	16	17	18	19	20
21	22	23	24	25	26	27	28	29	30
31	32	33	34	35	36	37	38	39	40

Outcome	Tally	Frequency
HH		
HT		
TT		

Are the results as you would predict?

____

____

Throwing Dice

Throw a dice 100 times and record the results below.

Number	Tally	Total
1		
2		
3		
4		
5		
6		

Record the dice throw **data** on the graph below.

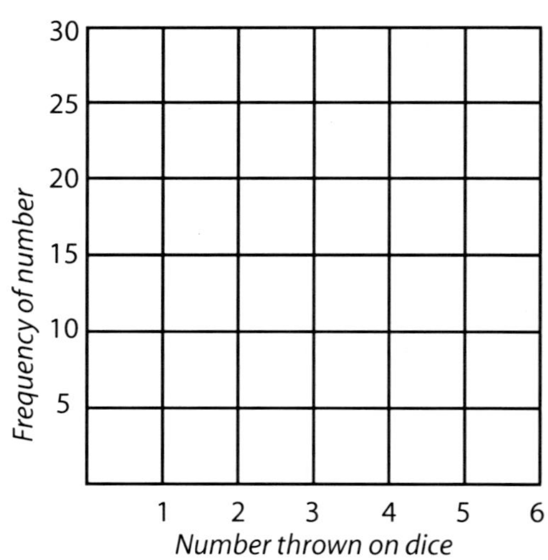

Is this what you expected?

____

____

2 Dice Game

Roll two dice 40 times. Each time add the numbers on the two dice and make a mark in the 'Tally' column next to the number that they add up to. After 40 throws, count up the total tally.

Number	Tally	Total
1		
2		
3		
4		
5		
6		
7		
8		
9		
10		
11		
12		

Why do you think some of the totals are most 'popular'?

____

____

____

Did you ever get a total of 1?

____

____

____

Card Cut

Take turns to randomly draw a card from a full pack of playing cards placed face down. Keep a tally of how many hearts, clubs, diamonds and spades you pick up. Repeat 50 times.

Suit		Tally	Total
Heart	♥		
Club	♣		
Diamond	◆		
Spade	♠		

At the end, sort the pack into suits and count how many cards are in each suit. Would you have expected the above result? ______________________

____

____

____

Probability Words

We use many different words to describe the probability or chance of things happening.

Here are two examples of words that we use.

1. There is a good chance it will rain today.
2. The odds are in favour of the horse winning the race.

Write down some more words that you would use to talk about probability.

____

____

____

____

____

____

____

____

Measuring Chance

info

If something is certain to happen we give it a probability of 1.
If it cannot happen we give it a value of 0.

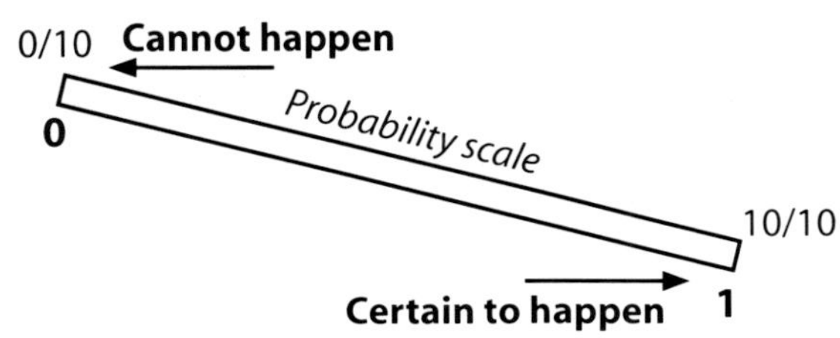

Estimate the chance of the following happening as a fraction out of 10.	
It will rain today	/10
You will go to bed today	/10
An alien will land in the garden	/10
A friend will phone you	/10
You will be given homework	/10
You will be given a job to do at home	/10

Picking a Lollie

g = Green
y = Yellow
r = Red
w = White
b = Blue
p = Pink

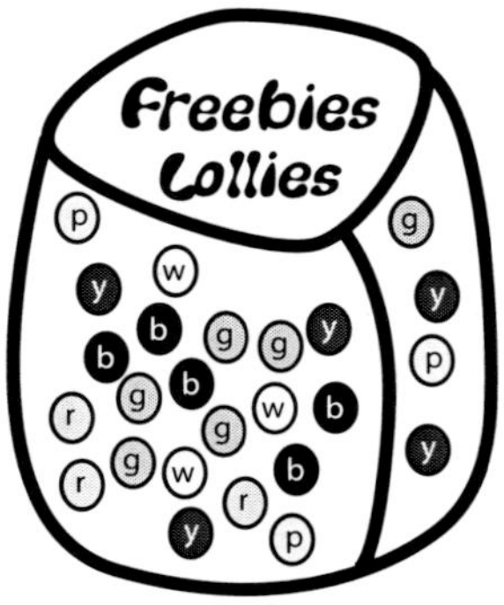

There are 25 lollies in this bag.

What is the probability of picking out the following?

A Green lolly	**6/25**	A Red lolly	
A Yellow lolly		A White lolly	
A Blue lolly		A Pink lolly	

Dice Numbers

Throw a dice 60 times. Record the number that turns up each time on the tally sheet. Add up your final tally for each number.

Number	Tally	Total
1		
2		
3		
4		
5		
6		

In theory, what is the probability of any one number turning up? ______________
Does your tally agree with the theory exactly? ______________________________
Why not? ______________________________

____

Choosing Colours

Put 10 red counters
+ 5 blue counters
+ 2 yellow counters into a bag

What is the probability of drawing a red ______
What is the probability of drawing blue ______
What is the probability of drawing yellow ______

Without looking pick out a counter 60 times, making sure you put it back in the bag each time. Each time, record the colour on the sheet below. Add up the totals.

Colour	Tally	Frequency
Red		
Blue		
Yellow		

Are these results expected? Exactly?
Approximately? ______________________

____

____

Dice Probability

Imagine you are rolling a dice. What is the probability of rolling each of the following?

Write your answers as fractions.

Roll	Probability
A one	**1/6**
An even number	
An odd number	
A number less than 3	
A multiple of 3	
A number greater than 4	
Any number but 4	
A seven	

Choosing Cards

Work out the probability of choosing the following from a full pack of 52 cards. Write your answers as fractions.

Any Heart	13/52	An even number	
Any Ace		A red card	
A Club		Any card above 10 (Aces Low!)	
A Jack		A picture card	
A Jack of clubs		A black card	
A 3 of any suit		Any King	
A 3 of Diamonds		A card between 5 and 8 (6 or 7)	
A Queen		A Queen or King	

Predicting Spin

You can spin the arrow around on the following circular board.

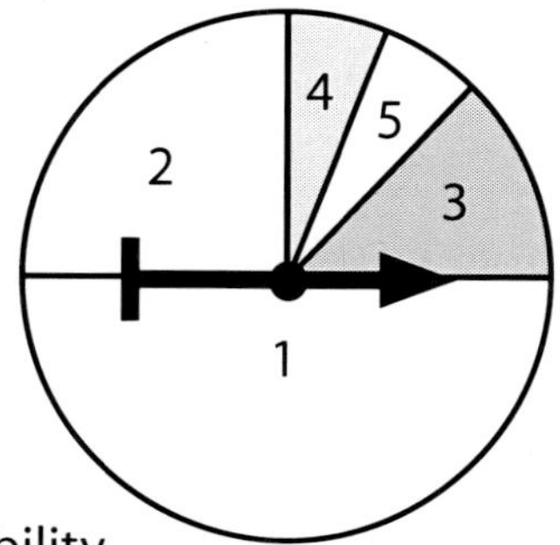

What is the probability of getting the following numbers? Write your answers as fractions.

1		4	
2		5	
3			

How many spins would you expect to make before you spin a 4?

____

____

Dice Combinations

If you roll 2 dice and add the total of the 2 numbers that you get, what is the probability of getting various different totals?

Fill in the grid below to help you work this out.

Dice 1 →

Dice 2 ↓

	⚀	⚁	⚂	⚃	⚄	⚅
⚀	1 2 1					
⚁						
⚂						
⚃					4 9 5	
⚄						
⚅			6 9 3			

Probability of a **2** 1/36 **3** ______ **4** ______

5 ______ **6** ______ **7** ______ **8** ______

9 ______ **10** ______ **11** ______ **12** ______

Alphabet Chance

You close you eyes and randomly point to a letter of the alphabet.

A	B	C	D	E	F	G
H	I	J	K	L	M	N
O	P	Q	R	S	T	U
V	W	X	Y	Z		

What is the probability of pointing to:

- a vowel ______________
- the letter **L** ______________
- a consonant ______________
- any letter in the word **PROBABILITY**

____

- any letter in your name

____

Surveys

info ***Surveys*** *involve collecting data.*

Think of 6 different groups of people or organisations that might use data.

____

____

____

____

____

____

Think of 3 things that you could survey at school.

____

____

____

Sampling

info *A* ***census*** *involves a survey of a whole population.*

A survey of a ***random sample*** *of a population involves a small fraction of the total population. The people (or things) involved should be chosen randomly, which means that every person (or item) in the population should have an equal chance of being chosen. Certain groups are not given preference.*

How could you get a random sample of:

1. Supermarket Shoppers? ______________________________

____

____

2. Library users? ______________________________

____

____

____

____

Food Survey

Write down the name of 2 popular foods allowed for sale at the canteen.

1. Food ______________________________

Results ______________________________

____

____

2. Food ______________________________

Results ______________________________

____

____

Ask class members which they prefer. For each answer you get, put a tally mark next to the preferred food above.

Discuss the results with the rest of the group. How would you go about doing a food survey for the whole school?

Taking a Tally

4 1 3 2 1 2 4 2 1 2 1 5 3 1 2
4 1 5 3 4 4
4 1 3 1 4 3 1 1 1 1
2 1 2 1 2 1 2 1 2 4 1 3 4 4 1 5 2

Count how many times each number occurs above. As you count each number, cross it off and make a mark next to that number in the tally sheet below.
Which number turns up most often?

Number	Tally	Total
1		
2		
3		
4		
5		

Use of Letters

Investigate which letters are used most commonly.

To do this, count the letters used in the paragraph below. For each letter, make a mark in the tally sheet alongside *(keep your tally strokes small)*. To help with the counting, each time you reach a total of 5 record it as:

| = one || = two ||| = three |||| = four ~~||||~~ = five

> "Once there were four children whose names were Peter, Susan, Edmund and Lucy. This story is about something that happened to them when they were sent away from London during the war because of air raids."

Quote from "The Lion, the Witch and the Wardrobe" by C.S. Lewis.

Count up the total for each letter.
Which letters are the most common?

____

Which letters are not used at all?

____

	Tally	Total		Tally	Total
a			n		
b			o		
c			p		
d			q		
e			r		
f			s		
g			t		
h			u		
i			v		
j			w		
k			x		
l			y		
m			z		

Sorting and Presenting Data

A class of 30 gets the following results in a test out of 10. Take a tally of the results and construct a line graph of the results on the grid alongside.

3	7	6	5	7	6
6	7	8	9	10	8
9	6	5	7	4	7
4	7	3	6	8	5
7	6	7	8	7	4

Score	Tally	Score	Tally
1		6	
2		7	
3		8	
4		9	
5		10	

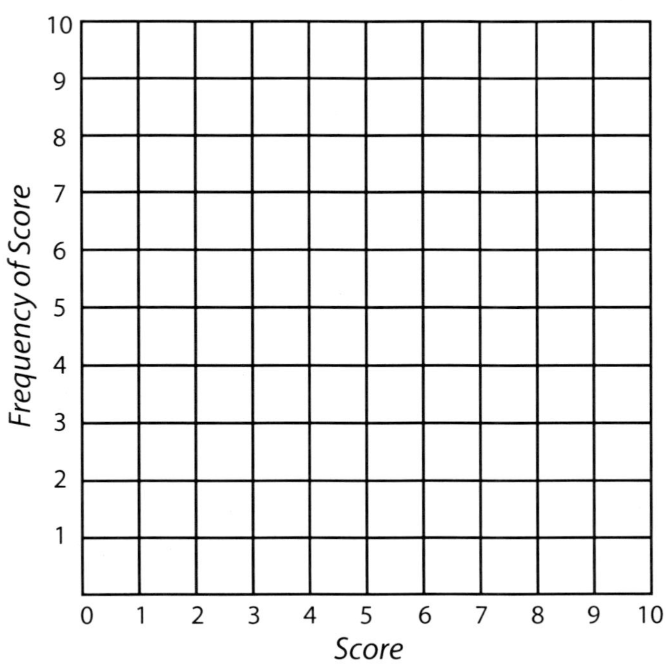

What was the most common score? ___________
What was the highest score? ___________

Picture Graphs 1

info *Using **picture graphs** is an easy and fun way to display data.*

Pies sold at a school canteen

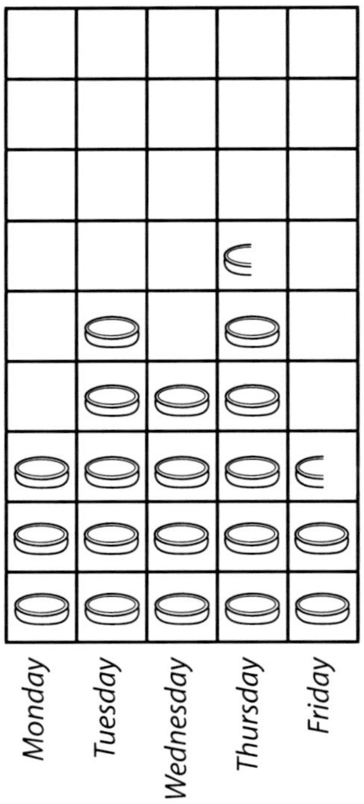

Scale:
= 10 pies

How many were sold on:

Mon ________

Tue ________

Wed ________

Thur ________

Fri ________

What was the week's total?

____

____

Picture Graphs 2

Movies hired out at a video shop

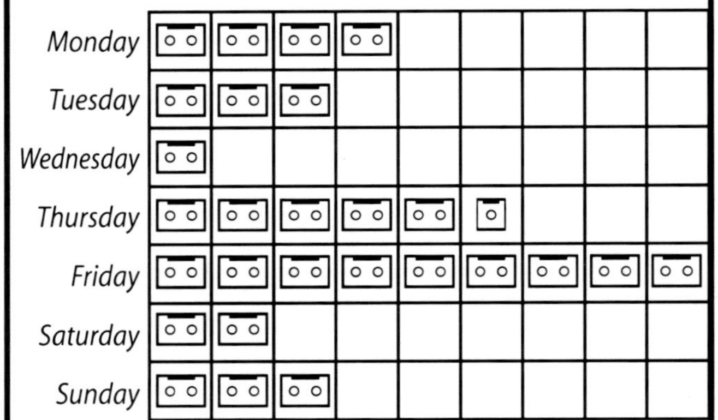

Scale: = 20 videos = 10 videos

How many were hired over the week?

____

What day were most videos hired?

____

Why so few hired on Wednesday?

____

Why so few on Saturday?

____

Pie Graph 1

A day at Camp Fabulous

Scale: Each sector represents 1 hour.

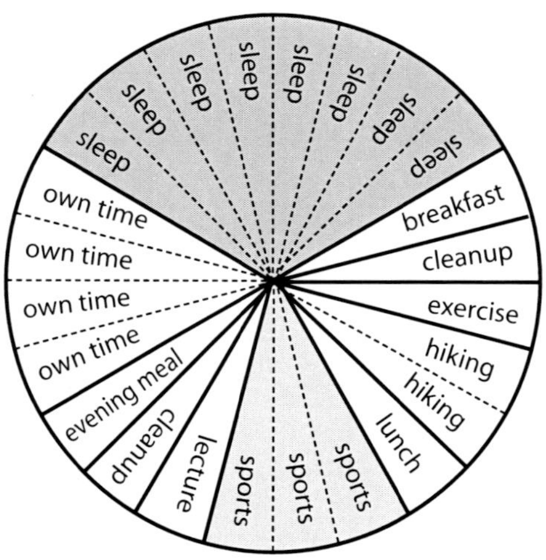

How long were you allowed to sleep? ______

How much time was given to hiking? ______

How much time was allowed for eating? ______

How much time was spent in cleaning up? ______

How much 'own' time was permitted? ______

Pie Graph 2

Use the Pie Graph to display how you spend your day. It is divided up into 1 hour sectors.

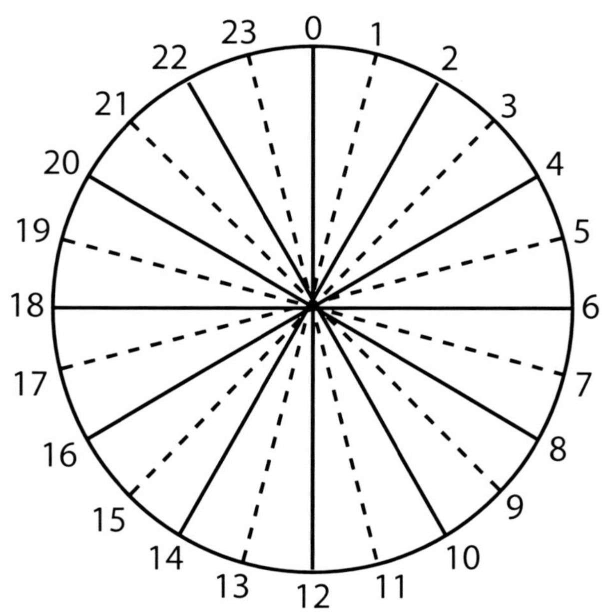

Bar Chart

An entire school of 900 students filled in a census on how they got to school on one particular day. The results are displayed in the a bar graph below.

Methods of travel

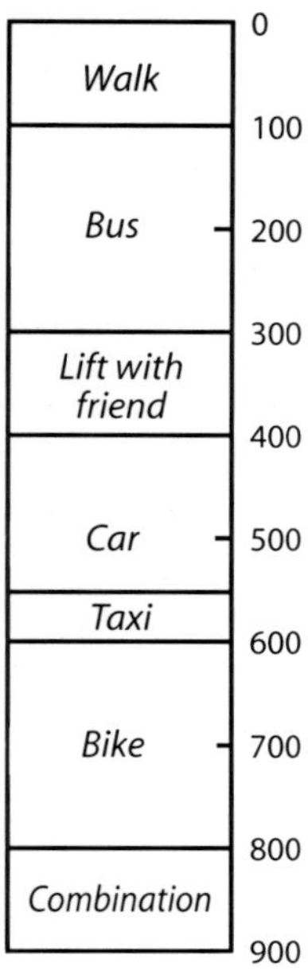

How many walked? ____________

Did more people use a bus in preference to a car? ____________

How many used taxis? ____________

Were there more walkers than bikers? ____________

Column Graph

info ***Column graphs*** *have a title, 2 axes and labels.*

Number of books read in a year

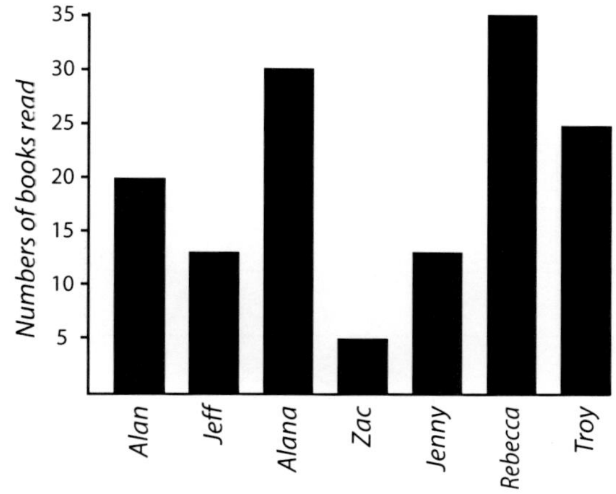

Who read the least? ____________

Who read 20 books? ____________

Who read the same amount as each other? ____________

What was the total number of books read by all? ____________

Histogram

info ***Histograms*** *are column graphs with no spaces between columns.*

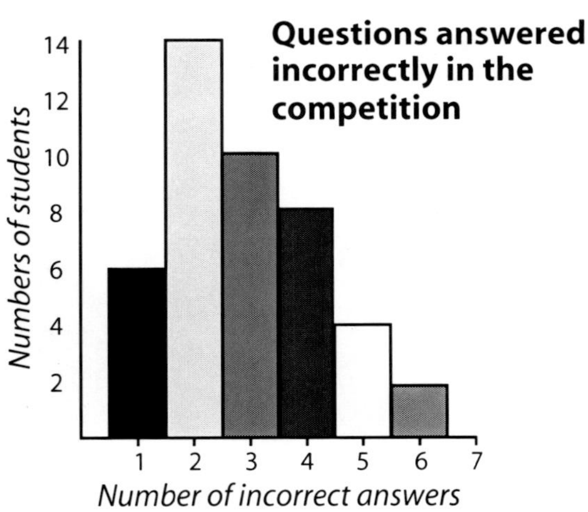

How many answered 4 incorrectly? ______

How many made more than 4 mistakes? ______

How many made less than 3 mistakes? ______

How many students entered the competition? ______

Line Graph

info ***Line graphs*** *show lines connecting points.*

Distance travelled on a bike ride

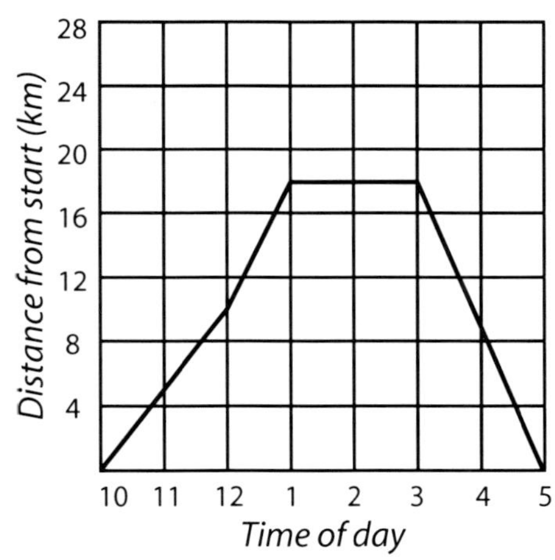

How far was travelled in the first 2 hours? ______

What was the speed in the next hour? ______

How long did the person rest? ______

What was the average speed on the return trip? ______

Data Range

info *The **range** of a set of numbers is the difference between the highest and lowest numbers.*

Find the range of the following.

1.	8	12	16	4	1	17	5	**17 - 1 = 16**
2.	1	3	7	4	2	7	8	
3.	76	41	62	19	38	79	5	
4.	1.2	6.4	3.7	4.4	7.8	3.5	0.1	
5.	0.6	0.4	0.1	1.2	3.3	5.0	4.7	
6.	−3	2	4	−1	6	8	−5	
7.	−1	−4	−8	−11	−2	−3	−5	
8.	£6	£1	£30	£9	£16	£4	£17	
9.	£0.25	£0.90	£0.80	£0.15				
10.	$\frac{1}{15}$	$\frac{3}{15}$	$\frac{12}{15}$	$\frac{8}{15}$	$\frac{6}{15}$	$\frac{5}{15}$	$\frac{11}{15}$	

Data Mode

info *In a collection of data the **mode** is the number that turns up with the highest frequency.*

Find the mode of the following.

1. 6, 2, 9, 2, 5, 5, 2, 4 **2**

2. 11, 15, 9, 12, 8, 12, 15, 12 ______

3. 1, 3, 6, 2, 6, 1, 6, 5, 7, 6 ______

4. 3.4, 3.1, 3.2, 3.1, 3.3, 3.5 ______

5. 112, 116, 113, 113, 110, 112, 113 ______

6. $\frac{1}{8}$ $\frac{2}{8}$ $\frac{2}{8}$ $\frac{4}{8}$ $\frac{5}{8}$ $\frac{4}{8}$ $\frac{2}{8}$ $\frac{4}{8}$ $\frac{3}{8}$ ______

7. 18, 16, 17, 16, 18, 16, 17, 17, 17 ______

8. 981, 980, 979, 980, 981, 980 ______

9. 64, 37, 64, 29, 47, 64 ______

10. 1, 2, 3, 3, 1, 1, 2, 2, 3, 1, 2, 2 ______

Data Median 1

info *When a collection of data is arranged from largest to smallest or smallest to largest the **median** is the score found in the middle.*

Example 2: 7, 3, 4, 9, 2, 5, 5
is sorted: 2, 3, 4, **5**, 5, 7, 9 giving a median of 5

Example 1: 3, 8, 4, 6, 5, 7
is sorted: 3, 4, **5**, **6**, 7, 8 giving a median of 5.5

Find the median of the following.

1. 4, 2, 3, 4, 5, 6, 9, 4, 6, 2, 5

______

2. 13, 8, 17, 19, 11, 14, 7, 12

______

3. 9, 11, 16, 12, 5, 7, 8, 7, 7

______

Data Median 2

Find the median of the following.

1. 6, 4, 3, 5, 5, 7, 8

______

2. 24, 26, 25, 26, 25, 25

______

3. 0.3, 0.7, 0.5, 0.6, 0.5

______

4. 1.5, 1.2, 0.9, 1.4, 1.0, 1.1

______

5. 107, 124, 111, 117, 119

______

6. 34, 58, 68, 51, 59, 70

______

Data Mean 1

info

*The **mean** of a set of numbers is the average. We get the mean by adding up all the numbers and dividing by the number of numbers that we have.*

Example: Four students obtained scores of 5, 6, 8 and 9 on a test.
There are four numbers, so the average or mean score was
$(5 + 6 + 8 + 9) \div 4 = 7$

Find the mean of 3, 6, 8, 4, 7, 5 and 4

Mean = ______________________

____

____

Data Mean 2

Find the mean of the following.

1. 4, 7, 8, 1

____

2. 6, 9, 10, 7, 5, 8

____

3. 3.1, 3.8, 3.6, 3.4

____

4. 62, 51, 58, 49, 55

____

5. 19, 23, 28, 21, 23

____

6. 0.5, 0.6, 0.8, 0.5

____

7. 13, 16, 14, 17, 8

____

Data Mean 3

Count the number of items in each of 6 boxes of drawing pins or paper clips. Record the results below and work out the mean.

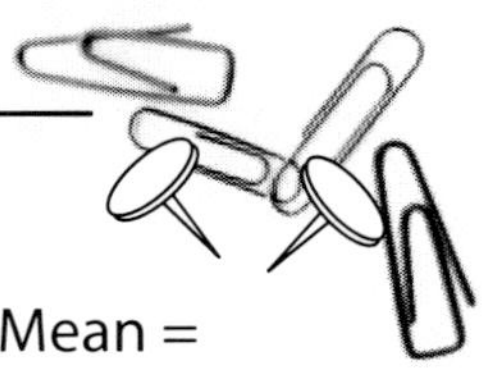

	Contents
Box 1	
Box 2	
Box 3	
Box 4	
Box 5	
Box 6	

Mean =

____

____

____

____

____

Does your figure agree with the "average contents" statement on the box?

____

____

Analysing Results

Work out a set of 10 questions to put to a group of students. Let the group answer them. Mark the answers.

Record how many were answered correctly here. ______________________

____

What is the **range**? (biggest score – smallest) ______________________

____

What is the **mode**? (score repeated most often) ______________________

____

What is the **median**? (in the middle when arranged from smallest to largest) ________

____

What is the **mean**? (total divided by number of items) ______________________

____

Data Collection and Analysis

Use the sheet below to record up to 35 items of data from any source that you choose. Then work out the range, mode, median and mean.

1. Results

Result	Score	Result	Score
1		19	
2		20	
3		21	
4		22	
5		23	
6		24	
7		25	
8		26	
9		27	
10		28	
11		29	
12		30	
13		31	
14		32	
15		33	
16		34	
17		35	
18			

2. Range
The difference between the lowest and highest score.

____

3. Mode
The number that turns up most often.

____

4. Median
The number in the middle when **all** the scores are written down from lowest to highest.

____

____

____

____

5. Mean (Average)
The total of all the scores divided by the number of scores (number of data items).

sum of all scores = ____________________

____

____

number of scores = ____________________

mean = ____________________

The Great School Car Park Survey

Do teachers drive gas guzzlers, bombs, sports cars or high performance sedans?
Find out by completing a survey of their cars in the school car park *(but do not touch any of the cars).*

Systematically walk through the car park and make a note of the type of cars.
Record how many of each type.

Car Make	Tally	Freq	Car Make	Tally	Freq

Remember: Complete a tally using the correct method.

This is correct. ~~||||~~ ~~||||~~ ~~||||~~ ~~||||~~ ||

This is not! | / | | \ | / | / | | \ | / | / | | \ | /

You could also collect additional information about each car, for example, the colour, how messy, how clean or how rusty.

Results of the Great Car Park Survey

Use the grid below to draw a graph to present your data.
You can use any type of graph.

Class Weight Survey

Survey the weight of everyone in the class.

Name (Go by a 'false' name if you prefer!!!)	**Weight (kg)**	**+ or – to show above or below the mean**

Mode = ____________________

Median = ____________________

Mean = ____________________

Which student is closest to the mean? ____________________

Stick Rules

Use matchsticks to construct the shape patterns below. Fill in the tables. For each table, work out the rule that gives the number of matches to make each shape. The first one has been done for you.

1.

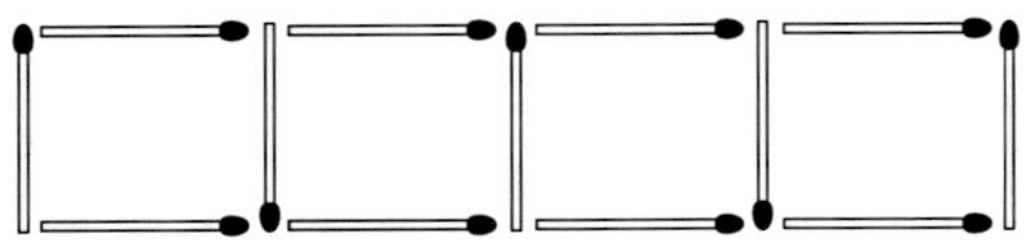

Number of squares	1	2	3	4	5	6
Number of matches	4	7	10	13	16	19
Number of matches = **3 x the number**						
of squares + 1						

2.

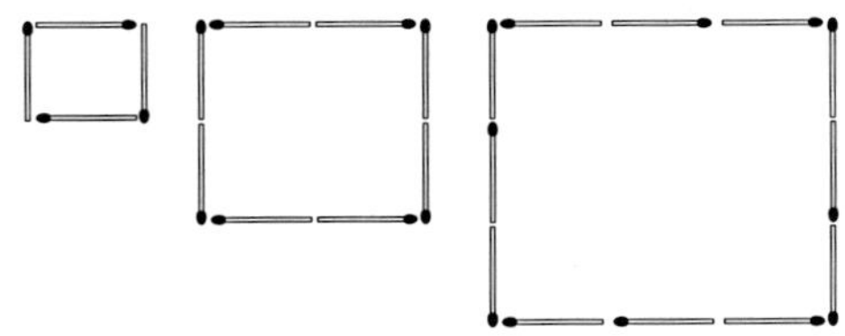

Length of side of square	1	2	3	4	5	6
Number of matches	4	8	12	16	20	24
Number of matches = **4 x the length of**						
sides of the squares						

3.

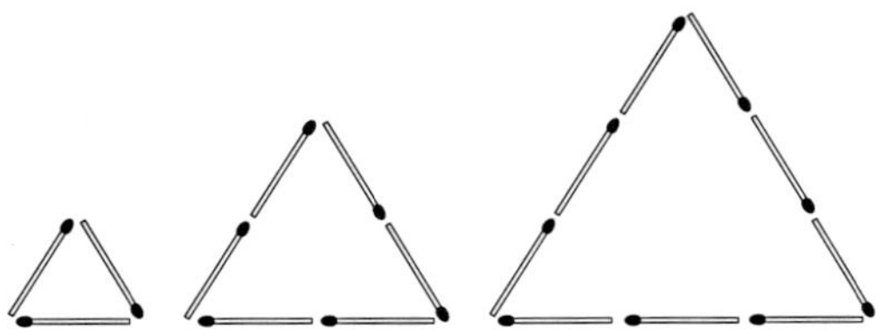

Length of side of triangle	1	2	3	4	5	6
Number of matches	3	6	9	12	15	18
Number of matches = **3 x the length of**						
sides of the triangles						

4.

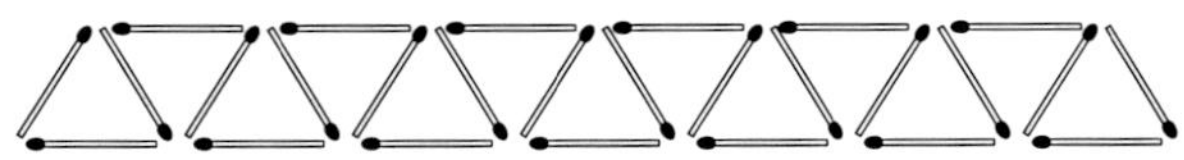

Number of triangles	1	2	3	4	5	6
Number of matches	3	5	7	9	11	13
Number of matches = **2 x the number**						
of triangles + 1						

5.

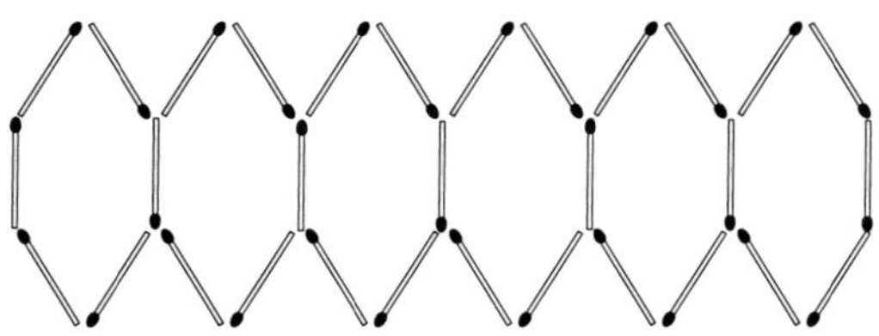

Number of hexagons	1	2	3	4	5	10
Number of matches	6	11	16	21	26	51
Number of matches = **5 x the number**						
of hexagons + 1						

6.

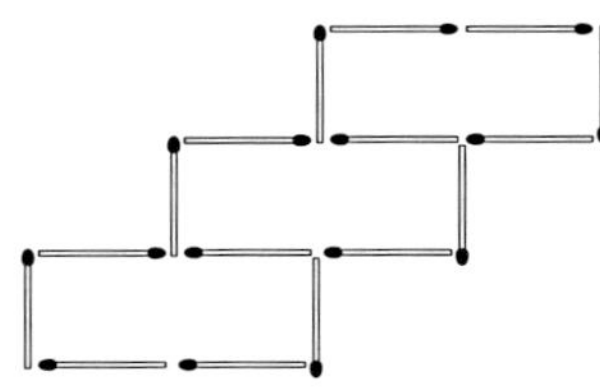

Number of rectangles	1	2	3	4	5	10
Number of matches	6	11	16	21	26	51
Number of matches = **5 x the number**						
of rectangles + 1						

7.

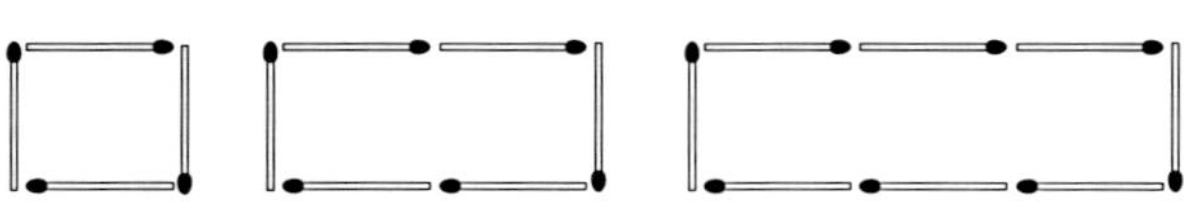

Length of long side	1	2	3	4	5	10
Number of matches	4	6	8	10	12	22
Number of matches = **2 x the length**						
of side + 2						

8. Design your own pattern
Example

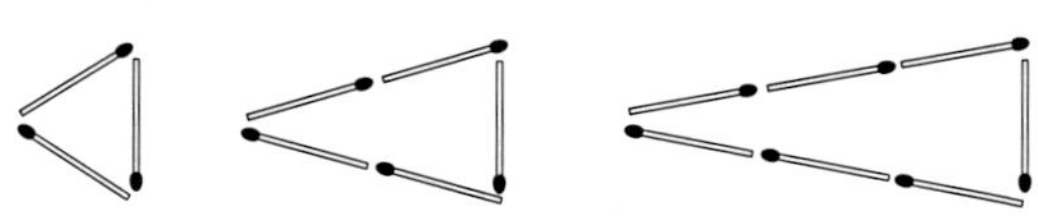

Length of long side	1	2	3	4	5	10
Number of matches	3	5	7	9	11	21
Number of matches = **2 x the length of long side**						

Finding Rules to Work Out Perimeter

Measure the length of each side of the shapes below and work out the perimeter of each. Then complete the rule.

1.

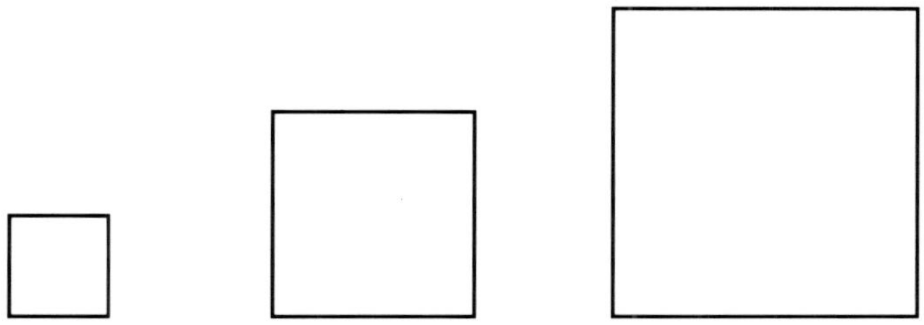

Side **1 cm** Perimeter **4 cm** | Side **2 cm** Perimeter **8 cm** | Side **3 cm** Perimeter **12 cm**

Rule:
The perimeter is **4x** the length of 1 side.
What length is the perimeter if each side is 22 cm?
Perimeter is **88** cm.

2.

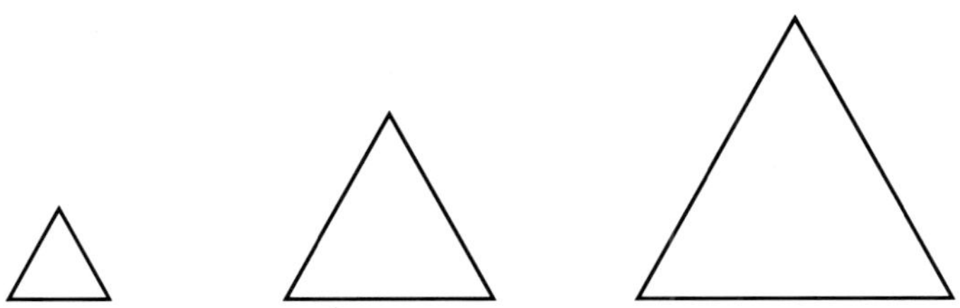

Side **1 cm** Perimeter **3 cm** | Side **2 cm** Perimeter **6 cm** | Side **3 cm** Perimeter **9 cm**

Rule:
The perimeter is **3x** the length of 1 side.
What length is the perimeter if each side is 41 cm?
Perimeter is **123** cm.

3.

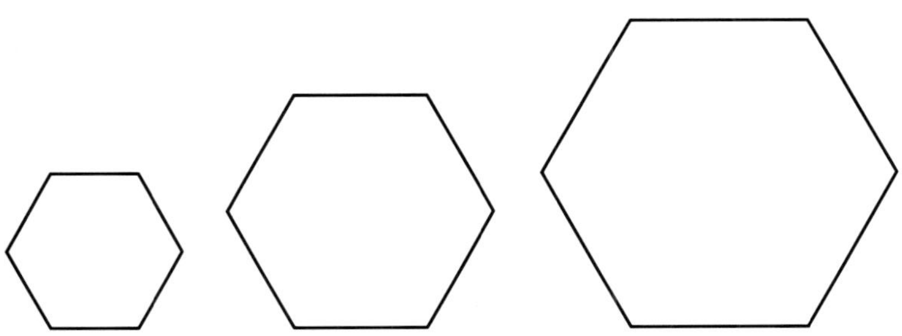

Side **1 cm** Perimeter **6 cm** | Side **1.5 cm** Perimeter **9 cm** | Side **2 cm** Perimeter **12 cm**

Rule:
The perimeter is **6x** the length of 1 side.
What length is the perimeter if each side is 67 cm?
Perimeter is **402** cm.

List some items here that have all sides of equal length.

Square Window Rule: **Perimeter is 4 x the length of one side**
Hexagonal table Rule: **Perimeter is 6 x the length of one side** ***Example***
Rule:
Rule:

A Rule to Build a Garden Path

Draw slabs around the shaded areas of garden below. Work out a relationship between the length of the side of the garden and the number of slabs needed to go all around the garden. The third garden has been done for you.

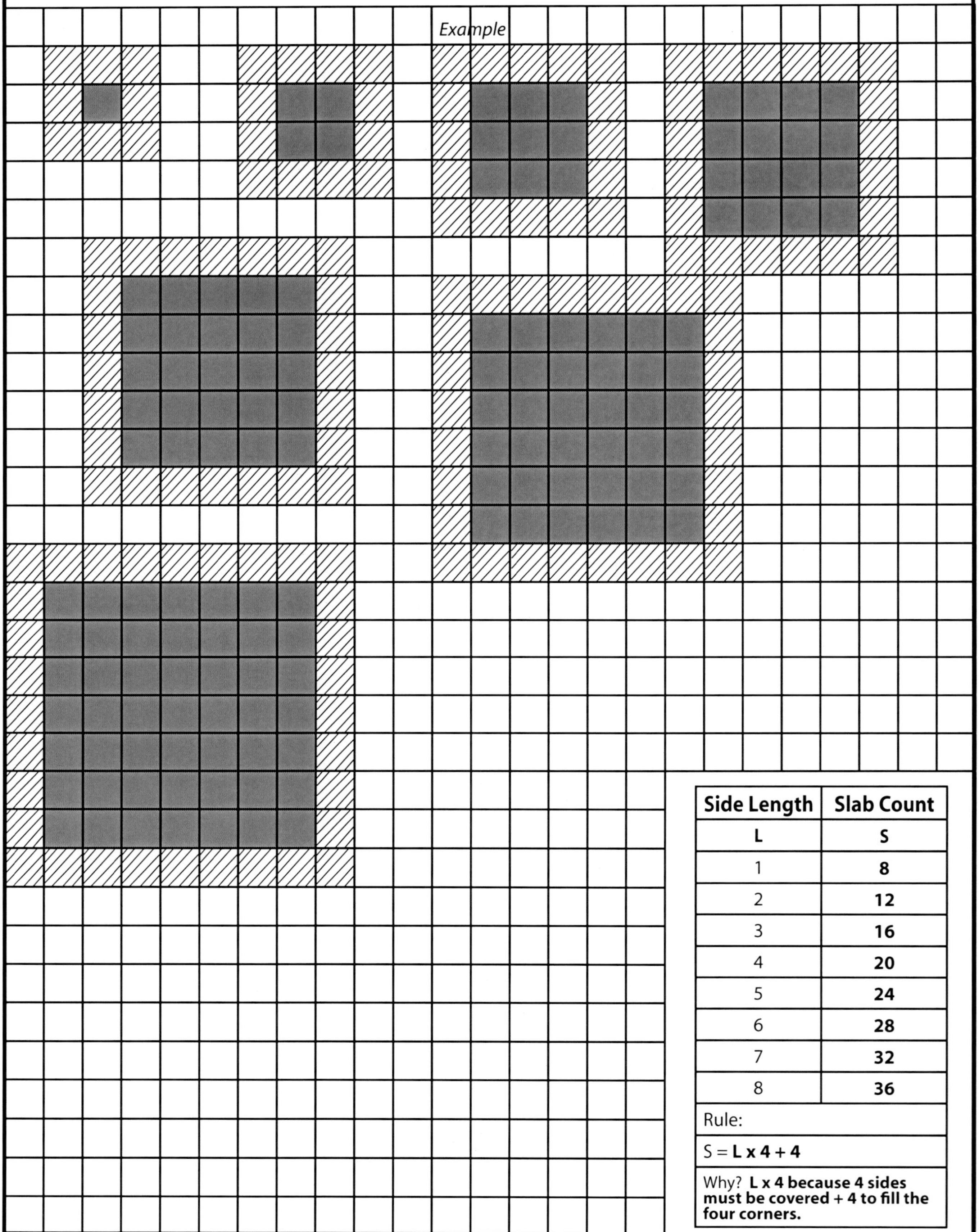

Side Length	Slab Count
L	S
1	**8**
2	**12**
3	**16**
4	**20**
5	**24**
6	**28**
7	**32**
8	**36**

Rule:

S = **L x 4 + 4**

Why? **L x 4 because 4 sides must be covered + 4 to fill the four corners.**

More Rules for Building Paths

Draw slabs around the shaded areas of garden below, as in the example. If L is the length of each garden, work out haw many slabs (S) you need to pave around each garden. What is the rule for finding the number of slabs in each of the three situations?

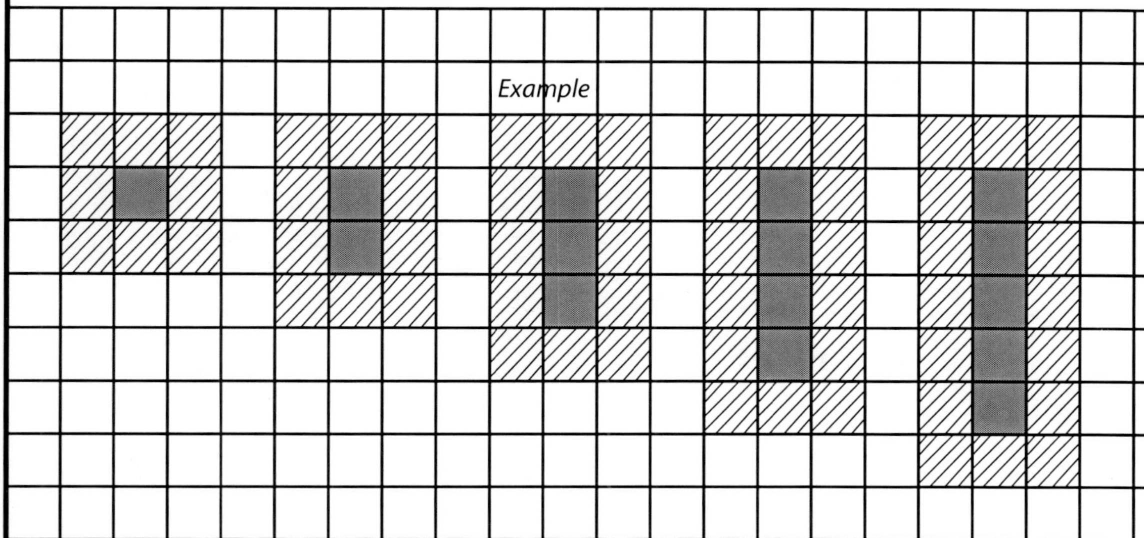

L	S
1	**8**
2	**10**
3	**12**
4	**14**
5	**16**
Rule:	
S=Lx2+6	

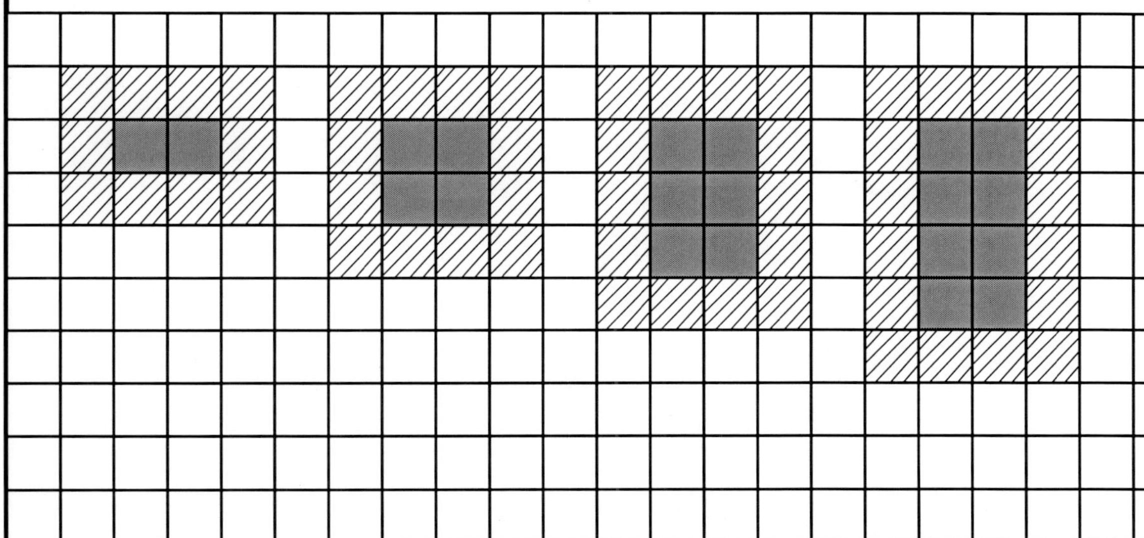

L	S
1	**10**
2	**12**
3	**14**
4	**16**
Rule:	
S=Lx2+8	

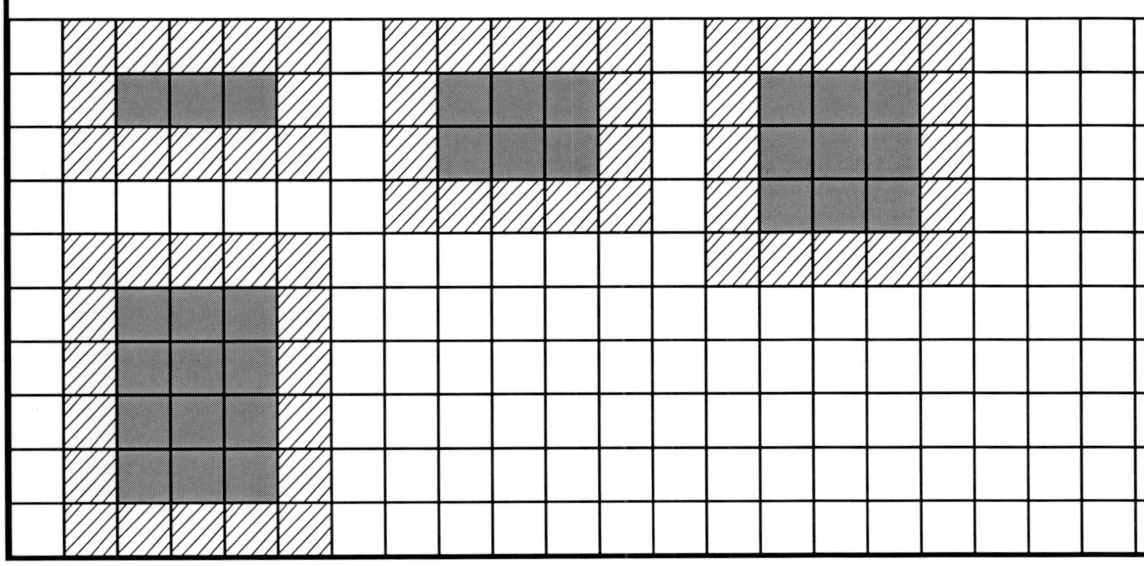

L	S
1	**12**
2	**14**
3	**16**
4	**18**
Rule:	
S=Lx2+10	

Searching for Rules with Circles

Use a ruler to connect every point (x) on each circle to every other point (x) on the circle. Record how many lines you draw in each circle. Think of a rule that lets you find how many lines you need to connect any number of points.

3 points need **3** lines

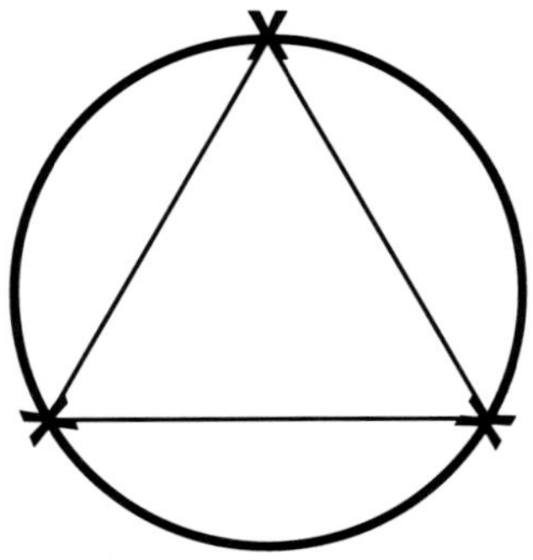

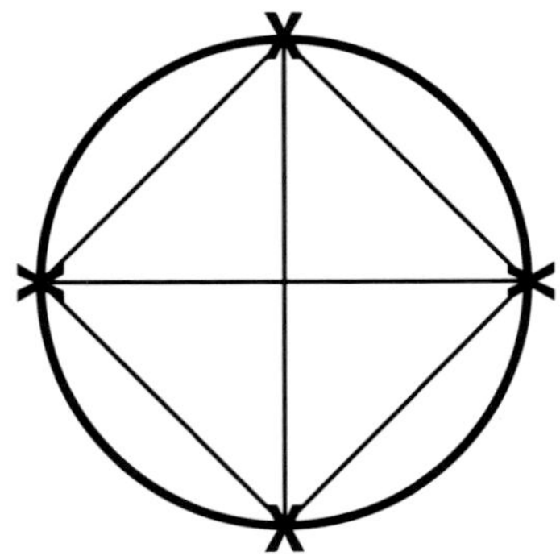

4 points need **6** lines

5 points need **10** lines

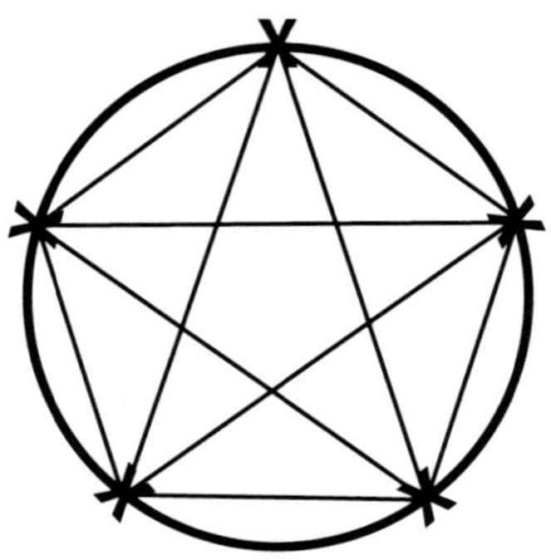

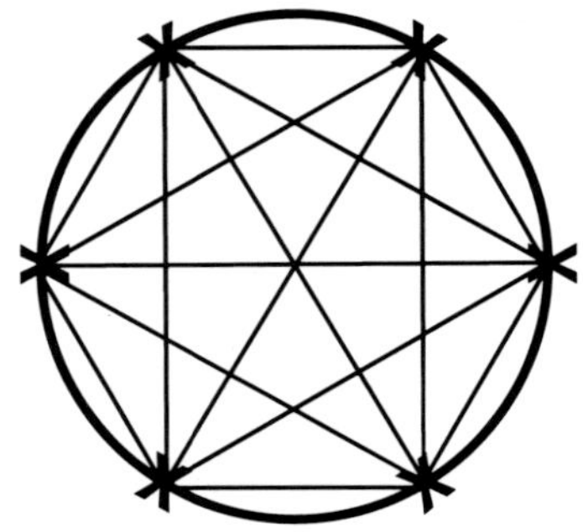

6 points need **15** lines

7 points need **21** lines

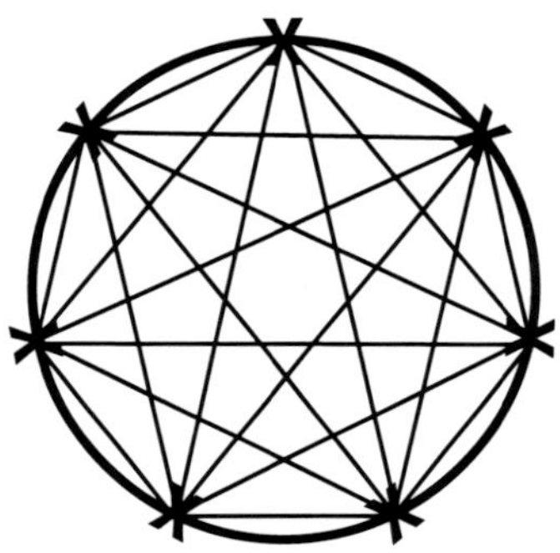

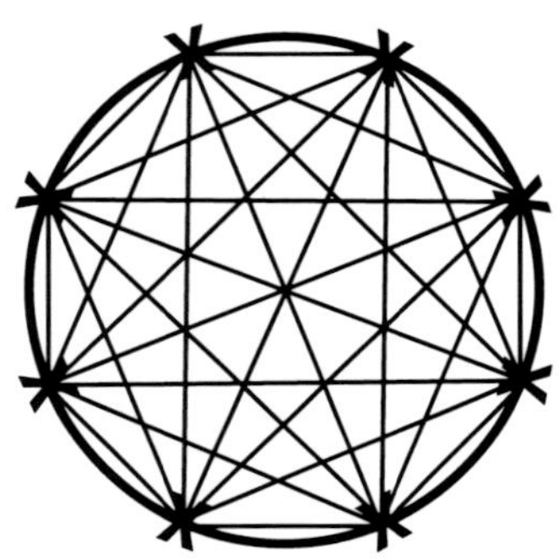

8 points need **28** lines

Number of Points	3	4	5	6	7	8	9	10
Number of Lines	**3**	**6**	**10**	**15**	**21**	**28**	**36**	**45**

Fill in the table above.

Find the rule to work out the number of lines needed to connect the points.

The rule is: **Number of lines = Number crosses on current circle x Number crosses on previous circle ÷ 2**

How many lines do you need to connect 9 and 10 points?

Completing Number Patterns

You often need to spot number patterns – both in the maths class and in life. Find the patterns and fill in the missing numbers below.

1.

1	2	3	4
5	6	**7**	8
9	10	**11**	12
13	**14**	15	**16**

2.

2	4	6	8
10	12	**14**	16
18	**20**	22	**24**
26	**28**	30	**32**
34	**36**	**38**	40
42	**44**	**46**	**48**
50	**52**	**54**	**56**

3.

1	5	9	13
17	21	**25**	29
33	**37**	41	**45**
49	53	**57**	**61**

4.

6	12	**18**	24	**30**	36	**42**	**48**	54	**60**	**66**	72	78	**84**	**90**	**96**	**102**

5.

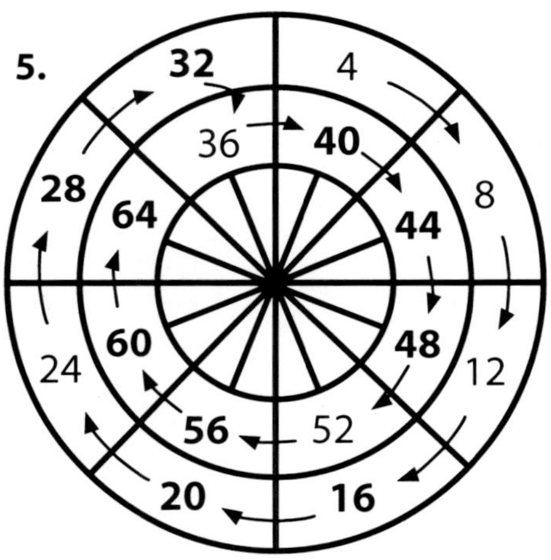

6.

2	3½	5	**6½**	8	**9½**	**11**
	20	18½	17	**15½**	14	12½
	21½	23	**24½**	26	**27½**	29
39½	**38**	36½	**35**	**33½**	32	**30½**

7.

1	2	4	7	11	16	22	**29**	**37**	**46**	**56**	**67**	**79**	**92**	**106**	**121**	**137**

8.

2	6	18	54	**162**	**486**	**1458**	**4374**	**13122**	**39366**	**118098**

9.

66	**64**	62	**60**	58	**56**	**54**	**52**	**50**	48	**46**	**44**	**42**	**40**	**38**	**36**	34

Design your own number patterns below. ***Examples***

10.

2.5	5.0	7.5	10.0	12.5	15.0	17.5	20.0	22.5	25.0	27.5	30.0	32.5	35.0	37.5	40.0	42.5

11.

100	90	81	73	66	60	55	51	48	46	45	45					

Following and Inventing Rules

Have a competition! Make a number follow the rules outside the boxes below and see if you all agree with the final number.

Examples	÷2	+10	×3	−20	÷4
4	= 2	= 12	= 36	= 16	= 4
	÷3	×2	+25	÷9	×20
3	= **1**	= **2**	= **27**	= **3**	= **60**
	×6	−12	÷2	×9	+19
3	= **18**	= **6**	= **3**	= **27**	= **46**
	−4	×4	+74	÷10	÷9
8	= **4**	= **16**	= **90**	= **9**	= **1**
	×4	×4	×4	×4	×4
4	= **16**	= **64**	= **256**	= **1024**	= **4096**
	+5	×2	−2	×5	+20
1	= **6**	= **12**	= **10**	= **50**	= **70**

Make up rules that start and end with the numbers below.
Have a +, -, x or ÷ rule for each square. Write the rules above the squares and the numbers they produce inside the squares as it is done above. *Examples.*

	x2	**x10**	**+5**	**+37**	**-0**
1	= **2**	= **20**	= **25**	= **62**	= 62
	x3	**-40**	**+1**	**+6**	**÷2**
31	= **93**	= **53**	= **54**	= **60**	= 30
	÷4	**+3**	**x2**	**+1**	**-42**
84	= **21**	= **24**	= **48**	= **49**	= 7

Working Out a Series from a Rule

Use the rules given below to work out the first 7 numbers in each series - let a=1, a=2, a=3, and so on. Also give the 10th, 27th and 40th numbers in the series. You can use a calculator!
All decimals are given to 3 decimal figures.

RULE	1st term	2nd	3rd	4th	5th	6th	7th	10th	27th	40th
1. a + 1	2	3	4	5	6	7	8	11	28	41
2. a + 9	10	11	12	13	14	15	16	19	36	49
3. 2a	2	4	6	8	10	12	14	20	54	80
4. 2a + 3	5	7	9	11	13	15	17	23	57	83
5. a + a + a	3	6	9	12	15	18	21	30	81	120
6. a/2	½	1	1½	2	2½	3	3½	5	13½	20
7. 10a	10	20	30	40	50	60	70	100	270	400
8. 3a -2	1	4	7	10	13	16	19	28	79	118
9. 3a –a	2	4	6	8	10	12	14	20	54	80
10. 4(a + 1)	8	12	16	20	24	28	32	44	112	164
11. 6(a – 1)	0	6	12	18	24	30	36	54	156	234
12. 5a + 4	9	14	19	24	29	34	39	54	139	204
13. 5(a + 4)	25	30	35	40	45	50	55	70	155	220
14. a^2	1	4	9	16	25	36	49	100	729	1600
15. $a^2 - a$	0	2	6	12	20	30	42	90	702	1560
16. a + 2a + 3a	6	12	18	24	30	36	42	60	162	240
17. a(a + 2)	3	8	15	24	35	48	63	120	783	1680
18. 12a – 7	5	17	29	41	53	65	77	113	317	473
19. a + ½	1½	2½	3½	4½	5½	6½	7½	10½	27½	40½
20. 3a – a/2	2½	5	7½	10	12½	15	17½	25	67.5	100
21. $a^2 / 2$	½	2	4½	8	12½	18	24½	50	364½	800
22. 1 – a	0	–1	–2	–3	–4	–5	–6	–9	–26	–39
23. 5 – a	4	3	2	1	0	–1	–2	–5	–22	–35
24. 1/a	1	1/2	1/3	1/4	1/5	1/6	1/7	1/10	1/27	1/40
25. a^3	1	8	27	64	125	216	343	1000	19683	64000
26. $\sqrt{a}$	1	1.414	1.732	2	2.236	2.449	2.646	3.162	5.196	6.325
27. 20/a	20	10	6.667	5	4	3.333	2.857	2	0.741	0.5
28. a(a-1)(a-2)	0	0	6	24	60	120	210	720	17550	59280

Working out Rules

All the boxes below perform an 'operation' on all the numbers coming in on the left hand side. Each number is changed and pushed out on the right hand side.

Inside each box, describe the operation performed by that box.
(Hint: The difference between outcome numbers gives the multiplication factor).

In	Rule Box 1	Out
1	Each number is	4
2	multiplied by 2	6
3	and 2 is added.	8
4		10
5		12
6		14

In	Rule Box 2	Out
1	Each number is	4
2	multiplied by 3	7
3	and 1 is added.	10
4		13
5		16
6		19

In	Rule Box 3	Out
1	Each number is	3
2	multiplied by 4	7
3	and 1 is taken	11
4	away.	15
5		19
6		23

In	Rule Box 4	Out
1	Each number is	1
2	multiplied	4
3	by itself.	9
4	(squared)	16
5		25
6		36

In	Rule Box 5	Out
1	Each number is	10
2	multiplied by 3	13
3	and 7 is added.	16
4		19
5		22
6		25

In	Rule Box 6	Out
1	Multiply the	1
2	number by 5	6
3	and take	11
4	4 away.	16
5		21
6		26

In	Rule Box 7	Out
1	You invent	**8**
2	a rule.	**14**
3	***Example***	**20**
4	**X6 + 2**	**26**
5		**32**
6		**38**

In	Rule Box 8	Out
1	You invent	**3½**
2	a rule.	**6½**
3	***Example***	**9½**
4	**X3 + ½**	**12½**
5		**15½**
6		**18½**

Chase the Rule

There is space to play 3 games below. In a game, every player gets to throw one dice 24 times. Write each number you get in one of the 24 squares in the game. Once a number is written it cannot be changed. If the two numbers you write for a rule meet the conditions of the rule, you score one point. When you have filled in all 24 numbers for a game, add up the number of points that you score. The player who scores the most points is the winner.

Keep a tally on your number of throws.	1	2	3	4	5	6	7	8	9	10	11	12
	13	14	15	16	17	18	19	20	21	22	23	24

RULE FOR THE POINT	**Write the rule with 'variables' a and b**	**GAME 1 *Examples***		**GAME 2 *Examples***		**GAME 3 *Examples***	
Sum of 8	a + b = 8	5	3	4	4	6	2
Difference of 3	**a – b = 3**	6	3	4	1	2	5
2nd double the 1st	**b = 2a**	1	2	4	2	3	6
Both numbers odd	**Both odd numbers a & b cannot be divided by 2**	1	3	3	5	5	1
Difference of 2	a – b = 2	6	4	3	5	3	1
Sum greater than 10	**a + b > 10**	6	6	5	6	6	5
Both numbers even	**a and b can be divided by 2**	2	4	6	2	4	6
One is 3 x the other	**b = 3a**	1	3	2	6	6	2
Sum is less than 4	a + b < 4	1	1	2	1	1	2
Sum of 10	**a + b = 10**	6	4	5	5	4	6
Product of 12	**a x b = 12**	2	6	3	4	4	3
One half the other	**a = ½b or b = ½a**	1	2	6	3	2	4
	Add up the score	**TOTAL**	12	**TOTAL**	12	**TOTAL**	12

Work Out Rules from Numbers

Look at the numbers in the columns marked A and B and see if you can find the rule to get from A to B. Write the rule underneath and complete the last two rows of B.

Clue: the difference between the numbers in successive rows of the B column is the number that the A values have to be multiplied by. ***But*** *also find out what else is done to the numbers.*

1.

A	B
1	6
2	8
3	10
4	12
5	14
16	**36**
20	**44**

B= A × 2 + 4

2.

A	B
1	11
2	15
3	19
4	23
5	27
20	**87**
50	**207**

B=A x 4 + 7

3.

A	B
1	3
2	4
3	5
4	6
5	7
13	**15**
24	**26**

B=A x 1 + 2

4.

A	B
1	4
2	9
3	14
4	19
5	24
18	**89**
25	**124**

B=A x 5 – 1

5.

A	B
1	10
2	14
3	18
4	22
5	26
17	**74**
32	**134**

B=A × 4 + 6

6.

A	B
1	5
2	12
3	19
4	26
5	33
26	**180**
28	**194**

B=A x 7 – 2

7.

A	B
1	2
2	7
3	12
4	17
5	22
30	**147**
50	**247**

B=A x 5 – 3

8.

A	B
1	7
2	15
3	23
4	31
5	39
100	**799**
200	**1599**

B=A x 8 – 1

9.

A	B
1	2½
2	3
3	3½
4	4
5	4½
11	**7½**
12	**8**

B=A x ½ + 2

10.

A	B
1	0
2	11
3	22
4	33
5	44
9	**88**
16	**165**

B=A x 11 – 11

11.

A	B
1	3½
2	6½
3	9½
4	12½
5	15½
6	**18½**
16	**48½**

B=A x 3 + ½

12.

A	B
1	12
2	14
3	16
4	18
5	20
17	**44**
54	**118**

B=A x 2 + 10

Following Rules

Follow the rule written on the box to work out what number comes out of it.

1.

N	N + 2
1	3
2	4
3	5
4	6
10	12
20	22

2.

N	N + 7
1	**8**
2	**9**
3	**10**
4	**11**
10	**17**
20	**27**

3.

N	(N×2) + 1
1	**3**
2	**5**
3	**7**
4	**9**
10	**21**
20	**41**

4.

N	(N×4) – 1
1	**3**
2	**7**
3	**11**
4	**15**
10	**39**
20	**79**

5.

N	(N+6) × 2
1	**14**
2	**16**
3	**18**
4	**20**
10	**32**
20	**52**

6.

N	(N×10) – 5
1	**5**
2	**15**
3	**25**
4	**35**
10	**95**
20	**195**

7.

N	N × N
1	**1**
2	**4**
3	**9**
4	**16**
10	**100**
20	**400**

8.

N	(2xN) +20
1	**22**
2	**24**
3	**26**
4	**28**
10	**40**
20	**60**

9.

N	(3×N) +5
1	**8**
2	**11**
3	**14**
4	**17**
10	**35**
20	**65**

If the left hand side **(N)** represents the number of hours that you work and the right hand side represents the number of pounds you will earn, can you decide which rule is the best one to work out your pay if you work for 10 hours? What about if you work for 3 hours?

Grouping Similar Items

In the diagrams below, count up all the similar items as shown in the example.
Grouping activities can be carried out with real items.

Button Key Button Key Key Key Key Key Button Button Key Key Button

Total is 8 keys and 5 buttons

Total is 10 circles and 6 triangles

A B A B A A A B A A B B B

Total is 7 A's and 6 B's

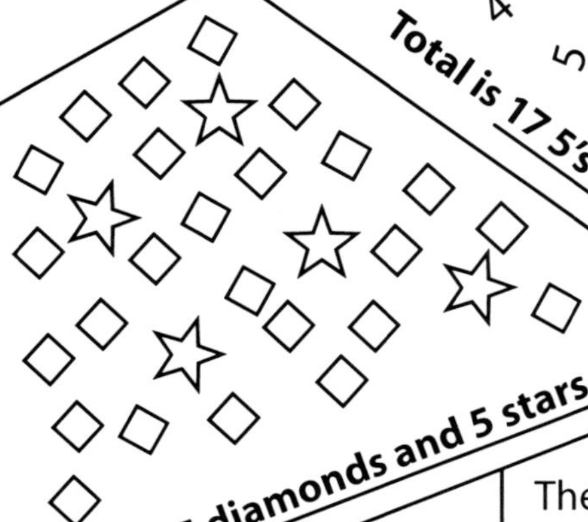

Total is 25 diamonds and 5 stars

4 5 4 5 4 5 5 5 4 5 5 4 5 4 5 4 5 5 4 5 5 5 4 5 5 5 4 5

Total is 17 5's and 11 4's

Total is 10 apples and 5 bananas

Total is 5 1's and 11 2's

The number of chocolates in each box is written on the chocolate boxes.
Is there a quick way we can add up the total number of chocolates?

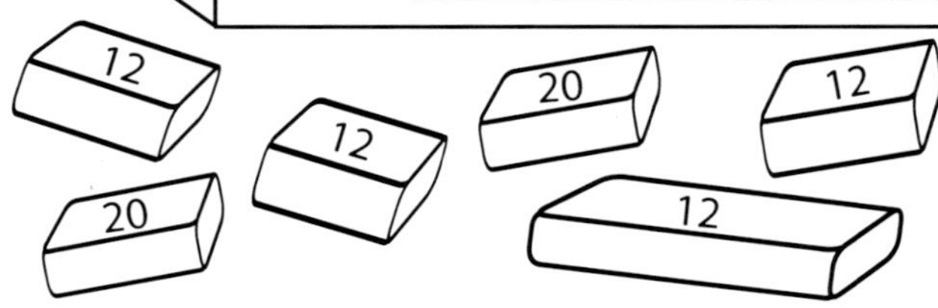

Total is 4 x 12 + 2 x 20 = 48 + 40 = 88

Bags of lollies.
How many lollies altogether?

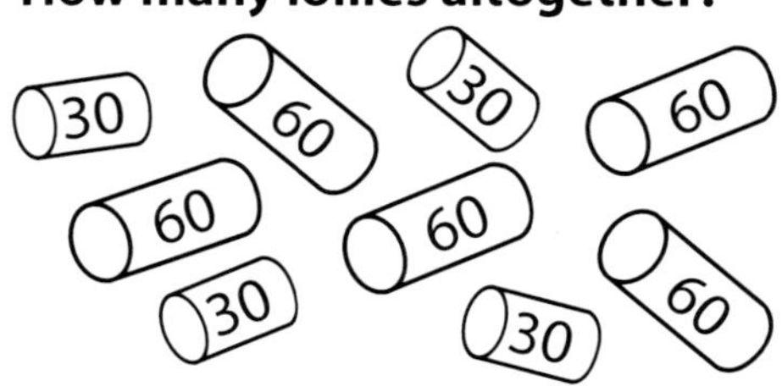

Total is 5 x 60 + 4 x 30 = 420

Green Black RED Yellow RED Yellow Pink Green Blue RED Yellow RED Black Pink Green Yellow

Total is 4 yellows + 3 greens + 2 blacks + 1 blue + 4 reds + 2 pinks

y y x z x z y x y z x y z z x x z y z x x y x x y

Total is
9 x's and 11 y's + 6 z's

Total is 8 x £5 + 5 x 50p = £40 + £2.50 = £42.50

Sorting Collections into Groups

Use wooden or plastic cubes, counters and pencils to practise sorting groups of items into smaller groups that each contain the same number of each item.

Example

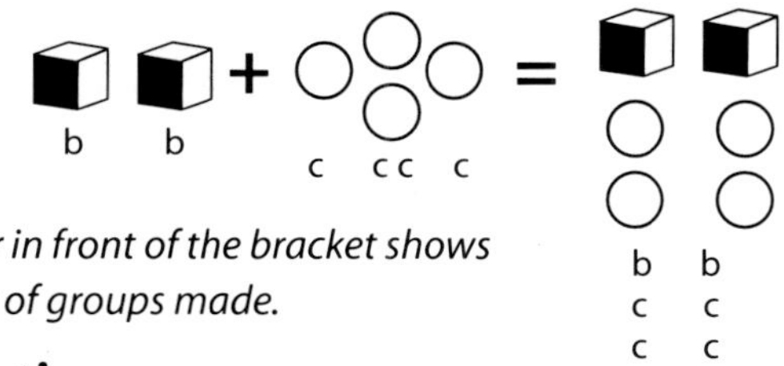

2b + 4c = 2(b + 2c)

b = blocks
c = counters

The number in front of the bracket shows the number of groups made.

Try the following collections:

1. 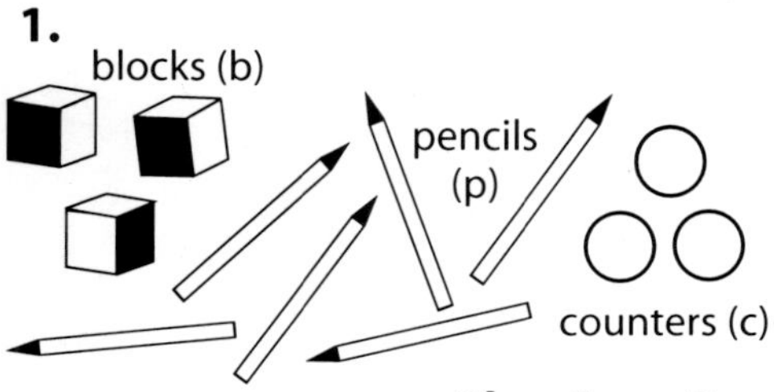 **3b + 6 p + 3c**	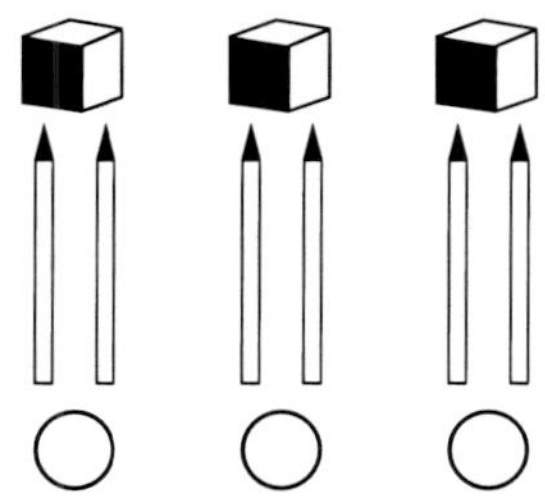 **= 3(b + 2p + c)** **(b + 2p + c) + (b + 2p + c) + (b + 2p + c)**
2. 6 p + 6c + 18b	**= 6 (p + c + 3b) or 2 (3p + 3c + 9b) or 3 (2p + 2c + 6b)**
3. 5c + 20b + 10p	**= 5 (1c + 4b + 2p)**
4. 2p + 10c +8b	**= 2 (1p + 5c + 4b)**
5. 7p + 14c + 21b	**= 7 (1p + 2c + 3b)**
6. 4p + 2c + 6b	**= 2 (2p + 1c + 3b)**
7. 3p + 3c + 9p + 3c Add similar items first.	**= 12p + 6c = 2 (6p + 3c) or 3 (4p + 2c)**
8. 11p + 11c + 11 b	**= 11 (1p + 1c + 1b)**
9. 5b + 5c + 3p *(Careful!)*	**Cannot be broken into even groups**
10. 2p + 2c + 12b	**= 2 (1p + 1c + 6b)**

Collecting Similar Terms

Consider the following.

Multiplying:	**Adding:**
8 x 2 = 2 x 8	*3 + 3 + 3 + 3 + 3 + 3 = 6 x 3*
3 x 6 = 6 x 3	*17 + 17 + 17 + 17 + 17 = 5 x 17*
20 x 5 = 5 x 20	*462 + 462 + 462 = 3 x 462*
So: a x b = b x a	*_ + _ + _ + _ + _ + _ = 6 x _*
And: ab = ba	***So: a + a + a + a = 4a***

Similar **or** ***like terms*** **can be collected together by adding or subtracting:**

3a + 7a + 4a + 6a	=	*20a*
17b – 11b	=	*6b*
xyz + 3xyz + 2xyz	=	*6xyz*
12xyz – 2xyz	=	*10xyz*
3ab + 2ba	=	*5ab*

Simplify the following.

1. 4a +5a + 6a + 1a = **16a**	**10.** 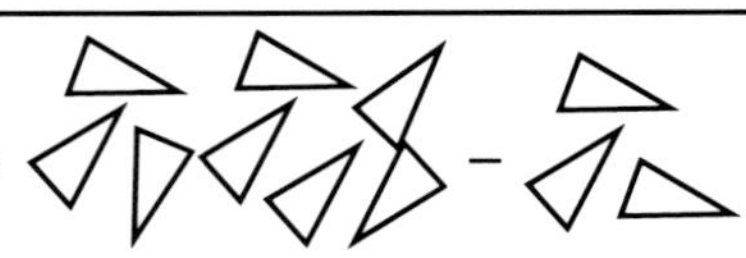 = 5◁
2. 11c + 9c + 4c – 2c = **22c**	**11.** 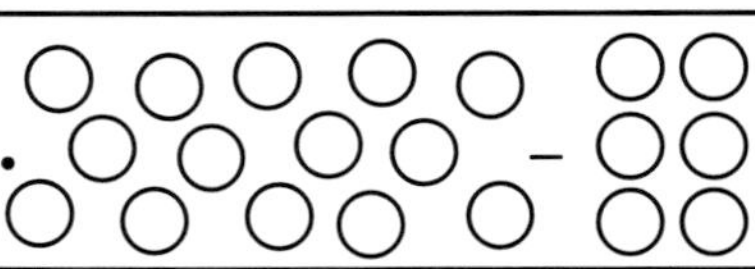 = 8○
3. d + d + d + d + d + 2d = **7d**	**12.**  = **8** □
4. ab + ba + 2ab + 7ab = **11ab**	**13.**  = **14**◁
5. 5y + 100y = **105y**	**14.** 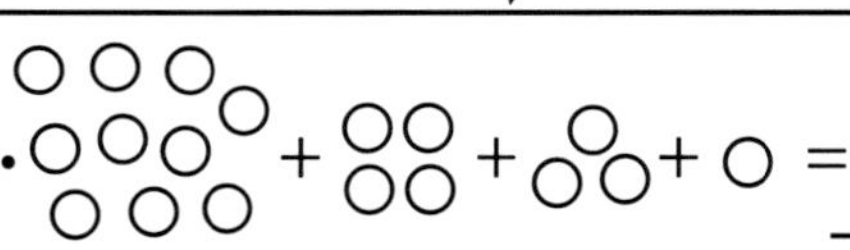 = **18**○
6. 12r – r – r = **10r**	**15.** c + 2c + 3c + 4c + 5c + 6c = **21c**
7. 35cd – 4cd = **31cd**	**16.** 13ab + 5ba + 7ab +2ab = **27ab**
8. 30a + 40a + 60a – 50a = **80a**	**17.** 428y + 20y – 15y = **433y**
9. 15f + 3f + 7f – 25f = **0**	**18.** 12b + 3b + 401b = **416b**

Collecting Like Terms

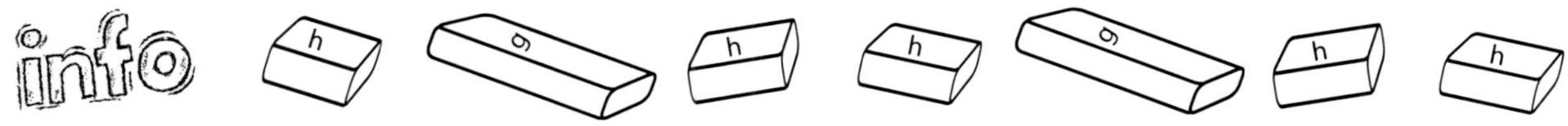

The large boxes above each contain **'g'** number of chocolates and the smaller boxes each contain **'h'** number of chocolates. To work out the total number of chocolates we have to collect all the 'similar' or 'like' boxes.

Our boxes could be written as	$h + g + h + h + g + h + h$
When we collect terms we get	$= 2 \times g + 5 \times h$
which we write as	**$= 2g + 5h$**

Collect the like terms in each question below.

1. $a + a + a + b + a + b =$ **$4a + 2b$**	**11.** $6e + e + e + 4f + f + 3f =$ **$8e + 8f$**
2. $3x + 3y + 7x + 10y + x =$ **$11x + 13y$**	**12.** $4x + 2x - x + 10y - 6y =$ **$5x + 4y$**
3. $10c + 3a + 10a + 21c + c =$ **$32c + 13a$**	**13.** $g + 2g + 4g - g + 11h - 3h =$ **$6g + 8h$**
4. $4a + 2a + 3a =$ **$9a$**	**14.** $6a + 8a + 2b =$ **$14a + 2b$**
5. $3a + 6a + 7b + 6b + c =$ **$9a + 13b + c$**	**15.** $100x + 100y + 100z =$ **$100x + 100y + 100z$**
6. $30w + 11x + 3x + y + 6y =$ **$30w + 14x + 7y$**	**16.** $30x - 3x + 15y - 6y =$ **$27x + 9y$**
7. $15a + 15b + c + d =$ **$15a + 15b + c + d$**	**17.** $200x - 17x + 3z + y =$ **$183x + 3z + y$**
8. $22x - 5x + 3y - 7 =$ **$17x + 3y - 7$**	**18.** $17j + 7j + j + 3xy + xy =$ **$25j + 4xy$**
9. $6p + e + 20f - 6p =$ **$e + 20f$**	**19.** $14j - 6j + 3k - 3k - 8j =$ **0**
10. $a + b + c + d + 4a + 3c + 12d + 2d + 3b =$ **$5a + 4b + 4c + 15d$**	**20.** $12b + 30b + 6 + c + d - 42b + d - 2d + 2d =$ **$c + 2d + 6$**

Writing Rules

Write a "general" expression for the following operations. The letter M represents any number.

1. Twice the number	**2 x M or 2M**
2. Half the number	**M ÷ 2**
3. The next consecutive number	**M + 1**
4. Four times that number	**4 x M or 4M**
5. The square of the number	**M x M or M^2**
6. The square root of the number	**$\sqrt{M}$**
7. Multiply the number by 2 and add 6.	**M x 2 + 6 or 2M + 6**
8. The difference between the number and 10.	**M – 10**
9. One fifth of the number.	**M ÷ 5**
10. What distance is the race? 	**M + M + M** **or 3 x M** **or 3M**

Give an expression for the sum of the following quantities.

11. M + M + M + M + M	**5 x M**
12. 6 + 8 + M	**14 + M**
13. A + B + B + B	**A + 3 x B or A + 3B**
14. x + y + 3	**x + y + 3**
15. 28 + M + M	**28 + 2 x M or 28 + 2M**
16. B + B + B +B + B + B	**6 x B or 6 B**

Give an expression for the difference between the following two quantities.
(The number on the left is the largest)

17. 20 and 17	**20 – 17**
18. M and N	**M – N**
19. 31 and x	**31 – x**
20. 100 and y	**100 – y**
21. P and Q	**P – Q**

Find a different way to write the following.

22. 5 + 5 + 5 + 5 + 7	**4 x 5 + 7**
23. a + a + a + a + a + a + a + b	**7 x a + b or 7a + b**
24. 3 x a	**3a or a + a + a**
25. x + x + x + x + y + y + y + y + y	**4x + 5y**

Calendar Problems

Example

Sunday	Monday	Tuesday	Wednesday	Thursday	Friday	Saturday
	1	2	3	4	5	6
7	8	9	10	11	12	13
14	15	16	17	18	19	20
21	22	23	24	25	26	27
28	29	30	31			

Add numbers to the above calendar so that it applies to the current month.
Look for patterns in the following way.

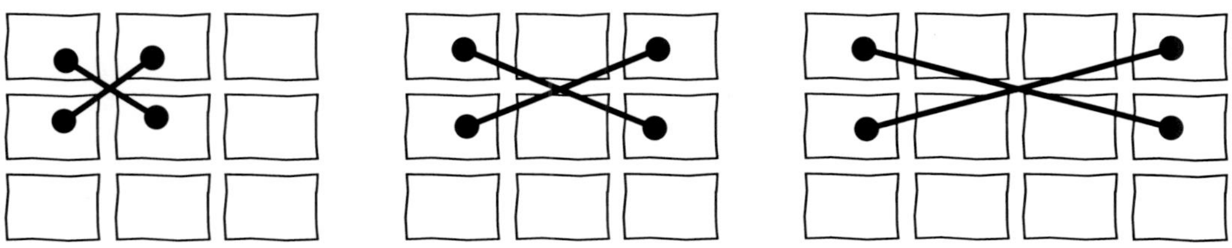

What do you notice when you add the diagonals in the above cases?
Opposite diagonals add up to the same number.

info

8	9
15	16

Pick on any four numbers that form a square on the calendar.
Notice that 9 x 15 – 8 x 16 = 7

Prove that b x c – a x d will always be 7.

a	b
c	d

b x c – a x d

= (a + 1) (a + 7) – a (a + 8)

$= a^2 + 8a + 7 - a^2 - 8a$

$= \cancel{a^2} + \cancel{8a} + 7 - \cancel{a^2} - \cancel{8a}$

= 7

a	b	=	a	a+1
c	d		a+7	a+8

In general terms

Working Out Perimeters

Work out a way to find the perimeter of each shape below and write this down using the letters. Then, use the actual numbers given for the letters to find the actual distance around the object.

1.

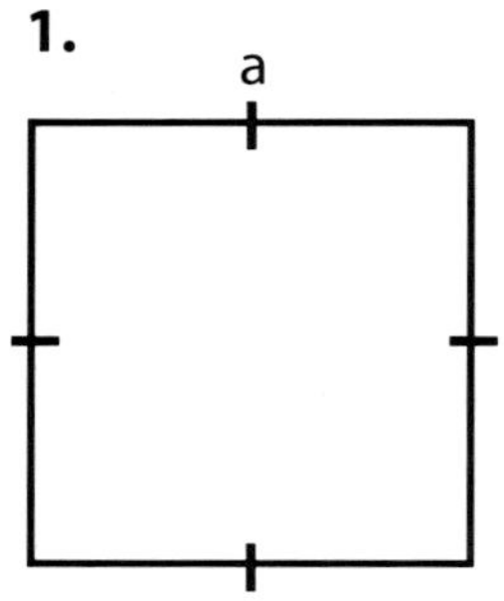

Perimeter (P) = **a + a + a + a**

If a = 2 cm

P = **2 + 2 + 2 + 2 = 8 cm**

If a = 7 km

P = **7 + 7 + 7 + 7 = 28 km**

2.

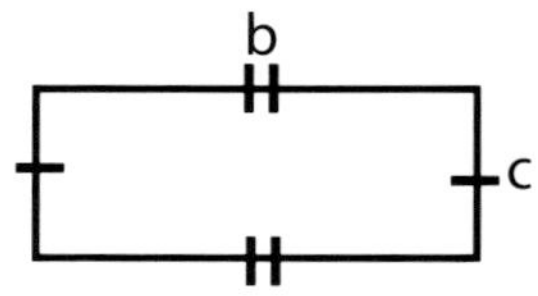

P = **b + c + b + c or 2b + 2c**

If b = 6 cm; c = 3 cm

P = **6 + 3 + 6 + 3 = 18 cm**

If b = 10 m; c = 2 m

P = **10 + 2 + 10 + 2 = 24 m**

3.

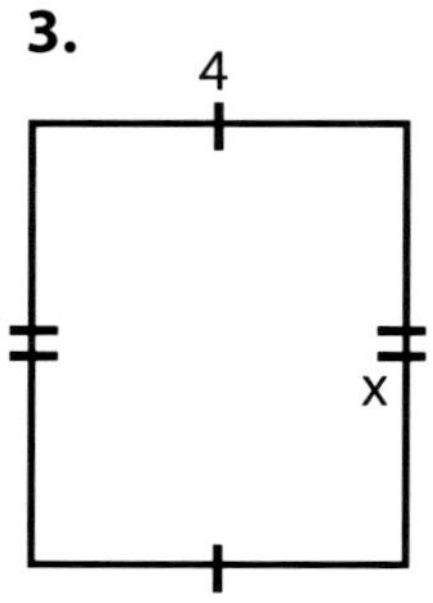

P = **4 + x + 4 + x**

If x = 31 m

P = **4 + 31 + 4 + 31 = 70 m**

If x = 15 km

P = **38 km**

4.

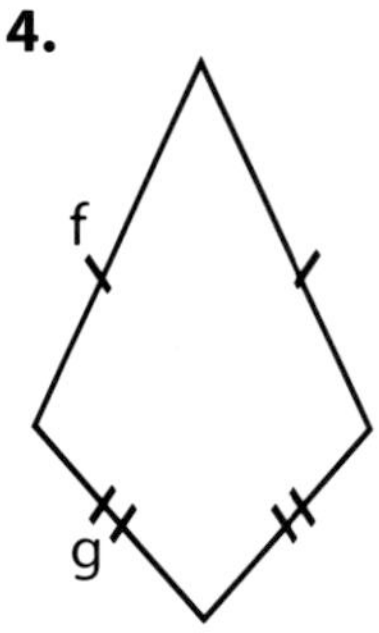

P = **f + f + g + g**

If f = 14 cm; g = 7 cm

P = **14 + 14 + 7 + 7 = 42 cm**

If f = 20 cm; g = 16 cm

P = **20 + 20 + 16 + 16 = 72 cm**

5.

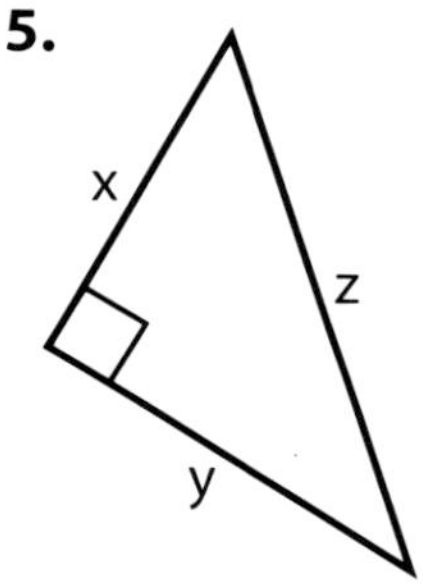

P = **x + y + z**

If x = 3 cm; y = 4 cm; z = 5 cm

P = **3 + 4 + 5 = 12 cm**

If x = 5 cm; y = 12 cm; z = 13 cm

P = **5 + 12 + 13 = 30 cm**

6.

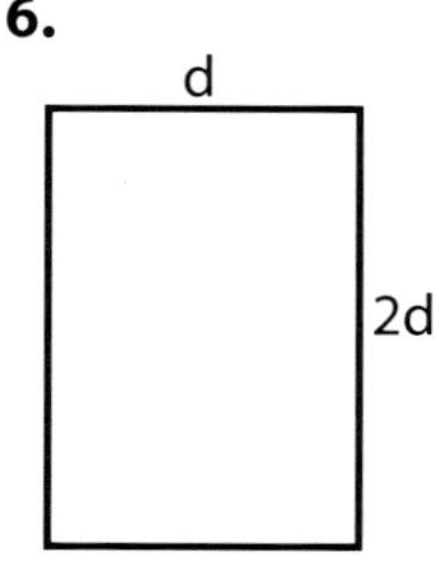

P = **d + 2d + d + 2d = 6d**

If d = 7 km

P = **6 x 7 = 42 km**

If d = 0.5 cm

P = **6 x 0.5 = 3.0 cm**

7.

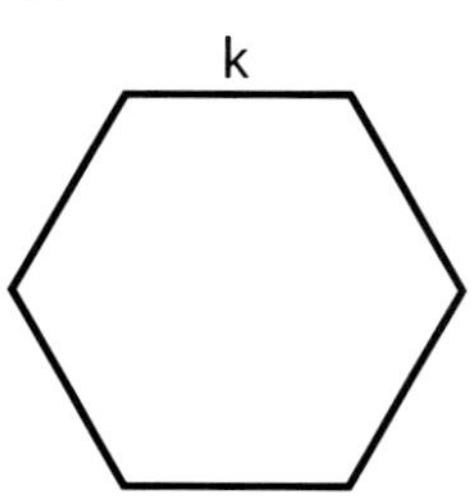

P = **k + k + k + k + k + k = 6 k**

If k = 3 cm

P = **6 x 3 = 18 cm**

If k = 1.6 m

P = **6 x 1.6 = 9.6 m**

8.

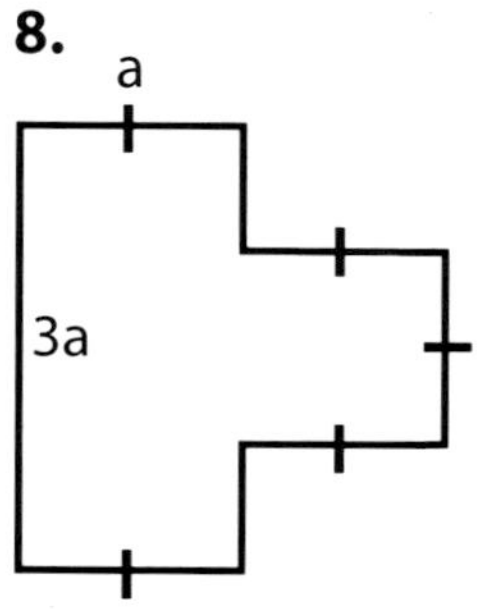

P = **3a + 7a = 10a**

If a = 5 cm

P = **10 x 5 = 50 cm**

If a = 22 m

P = **10 x 22 = 220 m**

9.

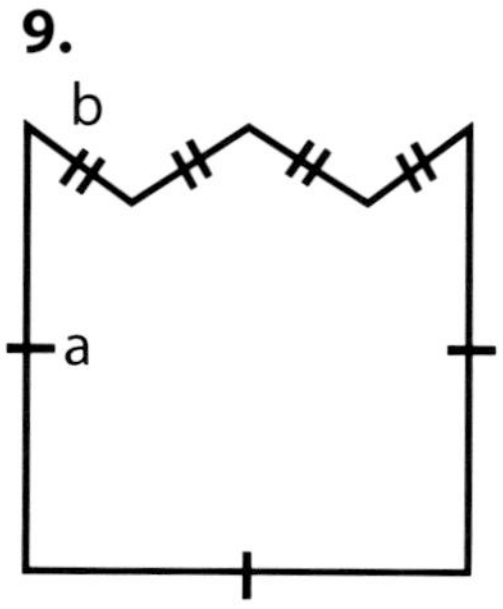

P = **3a + 4b**

If a = 9 cm; b = 2 cm

P = **3 x 9 + 4 x 2 = 35**

If a = 18 cm; b = 4 cm

P = **3 x 18 + 4 x 4**
= 54 + 16 = 70 cm

10.

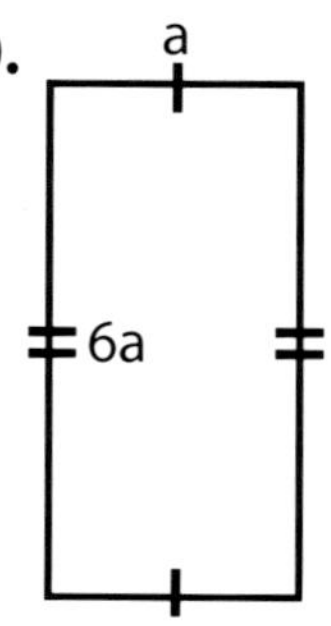

P = **a + 6a + a + 6a = 14a**

If a = 22 cm

P = **14 x 22 = 308 cm**

If a = 0.5 m

P = **14 x 0.5 = 7 m**

If a = 16 m

P = **14 x 16 = 224 m**

Solving Problems with Equations

Write an algebraic expression for the following statements and then find the solution. The first one has been done for you.

1. When 3 is added to this number the total is 14

$a + 3 = 14$ so $a = 14 - 3 = 11$

2. When I take 22 from the number I get 17

$a - 22 = 17$ so $a = 39$

3. When we double this number and take away 7 we get 29

$a \times 2 - 7 = 29$ so $a = 18$

4. A quarter of this number is 44

$a \div 4 = 44$ so $a = 176$

5. The square of this number plus the number is 42

$a^2 + a = 42$ so $a \times a + a = 42$ so $a = 6$

6. If you add 4 to this number and multiply the result by 9 you get 81

$(a + 4) \times 9 = 81$ so $a = 5$

7. If you double this number and double it again you finish up with 72

$a \times 2 \times 2 = 72$ so $a = 18$

8. The perimeter of this shape is 135 m long and consists of 5 equal sides, so how long is each side?

$a \times 5 = 135$ m so $a = 27$ m

9. If we double this number and then multiply it by 7 we get 70

$(a \times 2) \times 7 = 70$ so $a = 5$

10. A school of 16 classes has a total of 464 students. How large are the classes?

Class size = a so $16 \times a = 464$ so $a = 29$

Each line is 3 cm longer that the previous line. The total length is 385 cm. How long was the first line?

Length of all lines = $a+(a+3) + (a+6) + (a+9) + (a+12)$

$+ (a+15) + (a+18) + (a+21) + (a+24) + (a+27) = 10a + 135$

So $10a + 135 = 385$

$10a = 250$

$a = 25$ cm

Substituting Numbers and Letters

Use grouping symbols to write expressions for the following.

info *Example: Add 20 to the difference between 7 and 3 → **(7-3) + 20***

1. Take 50 from the total of 17, 12 and 100	**(17 + 12 + 100) – 50**
2. Add 10 to the square of 11	**(11 x 11) + 10**
3. Divide 62 by 31 and add 9	**(62 ÷ 31) + 9**
4. To the product of 6 and 2, add 3	**(6 x 2) + 3**
5. To the product of a and b, add c	**(a x b) + c**
6. Multiply 3 by 10 and take away 4	**(3 x 10) – 4**
7. Multiply a by b and take away c	**(a x b) – c**
8. Take 20 from the difference between x and y	**(x – y) – 20**

Find the numerical value of the following.
Let a = 8, b = 6, c = 4, d = 3
The multiplication sign is missed out to save room! 3bd = 3 x b x d, 3a = 3 x a etc.

1. a + b = **8 + 6** **= 14**	**2.** a x b = **8 x 6** **= 48**	**3.** a + b + c + d = **8 + 6 + 4 + 3** **= 21**	**4.** a + b – c = **8 + 6 – 4** **= 10**
5. c^2 = **4 x 4** **= 16**	**6.** 3bd = **3 x 6 x 3** **= 54**	**7.** (a + b + c) ÷ d = **(8 + 6 + 4) ÷ 3** **= 18 ÷ 3** **= 6**	**8.** (a – b) x (c + d) = **(8 – 6) x (4 + 3)** **= 2 x 7** **= 14**
9. 4a – bc = **4 x 8 – 6 x 4** **= 32 – 24** **= 8**	**10.** b x c ÷ d = **(6 x 4) ÷ 3** **= 24 ÷ 3** **= 8**	**11.** $a^2 - d^2$ = **8 x 8 – 3 x 3** **= 64 – 9** **= 55**	**12.** $3a - c^2$ = **(3 x 8) x (4 x 4)** **= 24 – 16** **= 8**
13. a + a + b + b + b = **8 + 8 + 6 + 6 + 6** **= 16 + 18** **= 34**	**14.** $(cd)^2$ = **$(4 \times 3)^2$** **(4 x 3) x (4 x 3)** **= 12 x 12** **= 144**	**15.** 3c + d = **(3 x 4) + 3** **= 12 + 3** **= 15**	**16.** 4a – 4b = **(4 x 8) – (4 x 6)** **= 32 – 24** **= 8**
17. (a + b) x 6 = **(8 + 6) x 6** **= 14 x 6** **= 84**	**18.** b x b x b = **6 x 6 x 6** **= 216**	**19.** c^3 = **4 x 4 x 4** **= 64**	**20.** abcd = **8 x 6 x 4 x 3** **= 576**

Finding Variables in a Rectangle

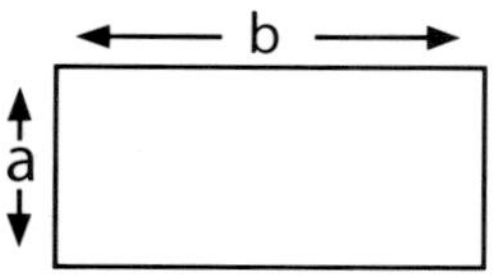

Imagine each square below has a side of 1 cm. Draw as many rectangles as you can of different sizes, but all with a perimeter of 36 cm. One side is represented by 'a' and the other by 'b'. Fill in the data sheet and see if you can see a link between a, b and the area of the rectangle (A).
To find the area, count the squares inside the rectangle. So the variables in the rectangle are - a , b and A. Perimeter (P) is a constant.

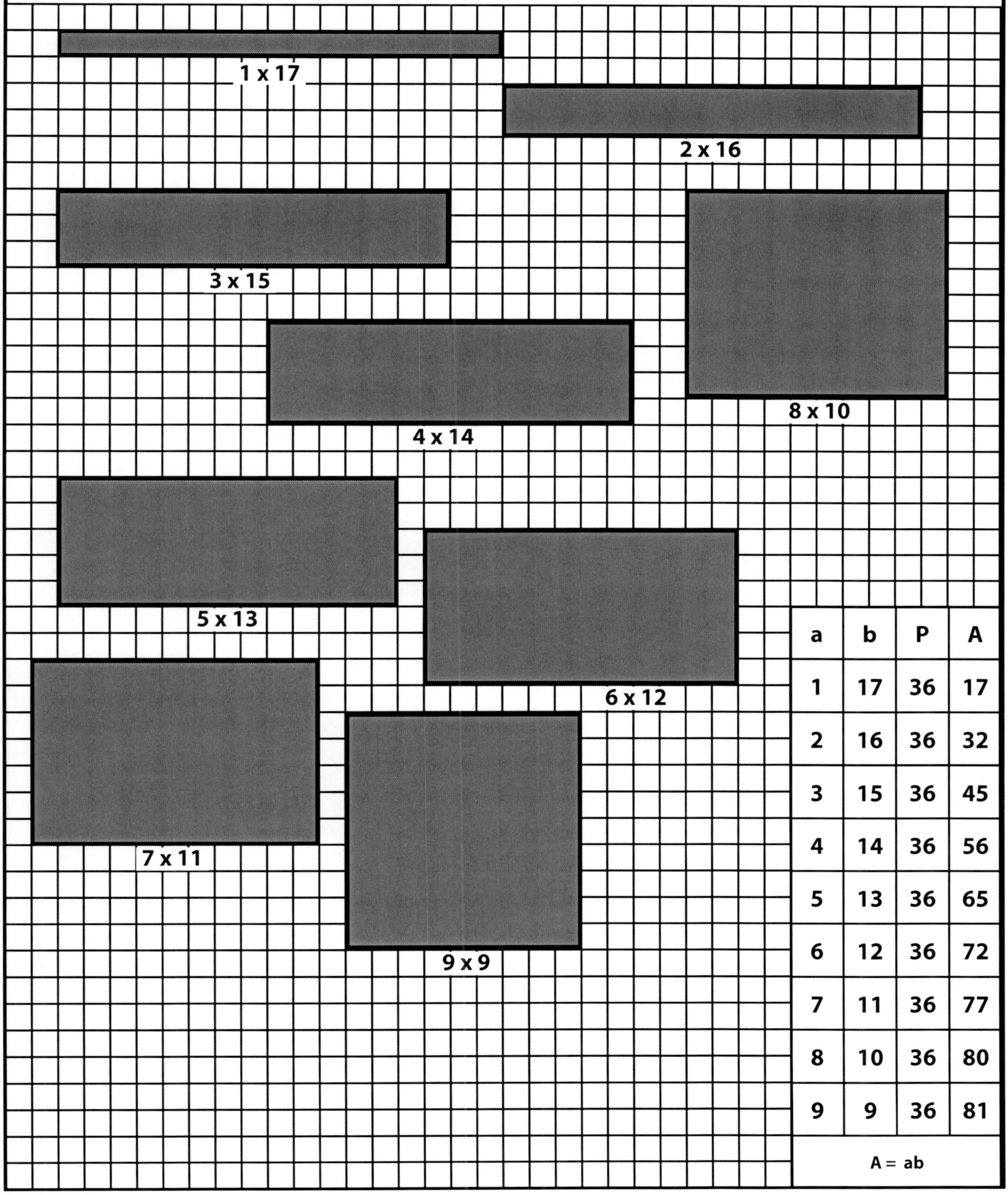

a	b	P	A
1	17	36	17
2	16	36	32
3	15	36	45
4	14	36	56
5	13	36	65
6	12	36	72
7	11	36	77
8	10	36	80
9	9	36	81
A = ab			

The Magic Square

info

In a magic square, all the numbers on the horizontal, vertical and diagonal lines add up to the same total. We can make such a square using three variables ***– a, b****, and* ***c****. Look at the way the letters a, b and c are organised in the square below.*

Work out that all lines do add up to the same total. Two lines have been done for you.

Diagonal (top left to bottom right): **a+a+a–b+b = 3a**

Column 1: **a+a+a+b–b–c+c = 3a**

Column 2: **a+a+a–b+b+c–c = 3a**

Column 3: **a+a+a+b–b–c+c = 3a**

Diagonal (bottom left to top right): **a+a+a–c+c = 3a**

a – b	a + b – c	a + c	**a+a+a–b+b–c+c = 3a**
a + b + c	a	a – b – c	**a+a+a+b–b+c–c = 3a**
a – c	a – b + c	a + b	**a+a+a–b+b–c+c = 3a**

Use the values of a, b and c below to fill in the numbers in the squares.
(You will have some negative numbers.)

a = 10 b = 8 c = 4

2	**14**	**14**
22	**10**	**–2**
6	**6**	**18**

a = 9 b = 6 c = 1

3	**14**	**10**
16	**9**	**2**
8	**4**	**15**

a = 5 b = 3 c = 4

2	**4**	**9**
12	**5**	**–2**
1	**6**	**8**

Graphing the Plumber

A plumber charges for house calls at the following rate:

$$c = 16h + 8$$

where c = charge in pounds and h = the number of hours worked

Work out a table of charges for working up to 8 hours.

Number of hours worked	Calculation	Charge (c) (£)
1	**c = 16 x 1 + 8**	**24**
2	**c = 16 x 2 + 8**	**40**
3	**c = 16 x 3 + 8**	**56**
4	**c = 16 x 4 + 8**	**72**
5	**c = 16 x 5 + 8**	**88**
6	**c = 16 x 6 + 8**	**104**
7	**c = 16 x 7 + 8**	**120**
8	**c = 16 x 8 + 8**	**136**

Plot a graph below of the amount charged compared to the number of hours worked.

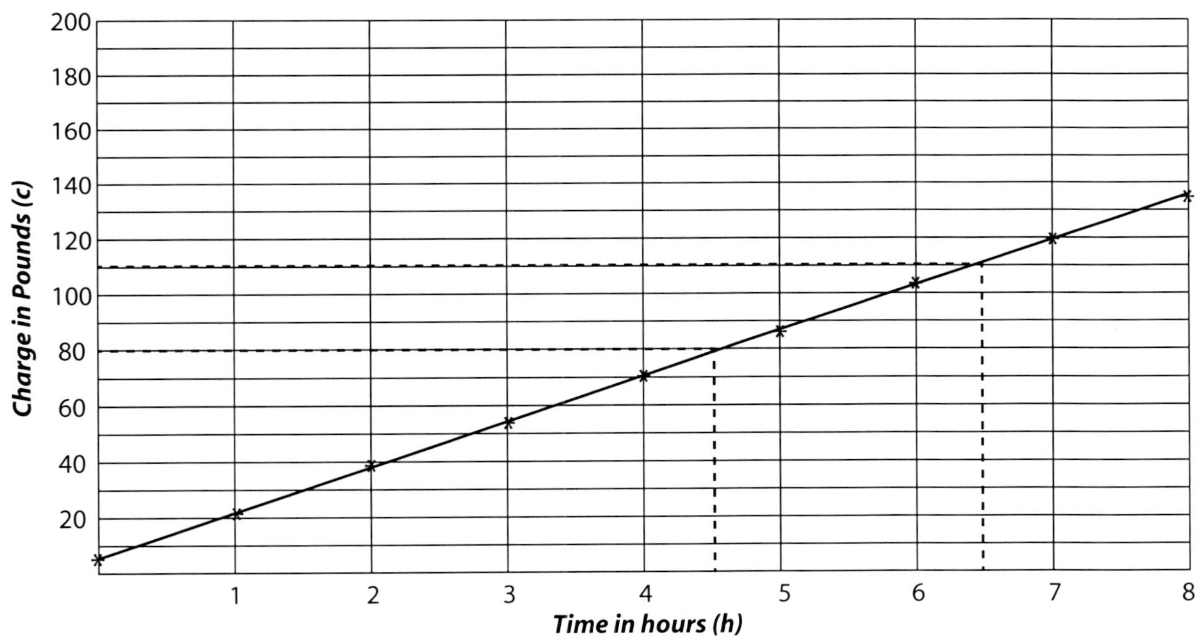

Answer the following questions.

1. How much does the plumber charge for 4 ½ hours work? **£80**
2. If the plumber charged £112 how long was the work period? **6½ hours**
3. How much is charged if 40 hours are worked? *(Use the fact that c = 16h + 8)* **£648**

Odds and Evens

Let **E** stand for any even number and **O** stand for any odd number.

Cut out the E's and O's and the x, –, +, – and = signs below. Then make up your own equations. For more challenging problems include the numbers 1 to 9 in the equations.

Examples:

E + 1 = O
E x 2 = E
E + 5 + E = O
O + E + O + E + O = O

Try:

E + O = **O**
E + E = **E**
O x 2 = **E**
4 x E = **E**

E	E	E	E	E	E	E	E	E	E
O	O	O	O	O	O	O	O	O	O
X	X	X	X	÷	÷	÷	÷	+	+
+	+	–	–	+	+	=	=	=	=
10	20	30	40	1	2	3	4	5	6
7	8	9	1	2	3	4	5	6	7
8	9	1	2	3	4	5	6	7	8
9	1	2	3	4	5	6	7	8	9

Set problems for other people and ask them to find if the answer is an odd number or an even number.

Spotting Patterns 1

Use counters or pieces of paper to find triangular and square numbers.

Square numbers

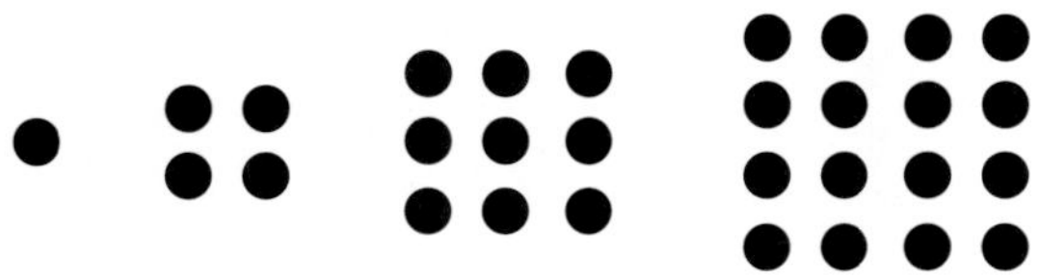

Find 4 more square numbers

25 **36** **49** **64**

Triangular numbers

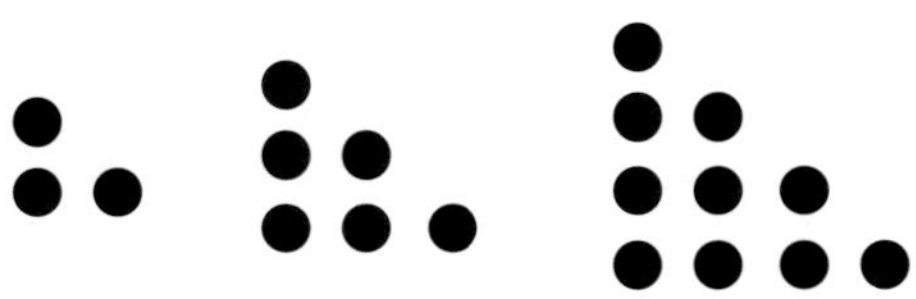

Find 4 more triangular numbers

15 **21** **28** **36**

Spotting Patterns 2

Find the next 4 numbers in the series below.

1	2	3	4	**5**	**6**	**7**	**8**
2	4	6	8	**10**	**12**	**14**	**16**
1	5	9	13	**17**	**21**	**25**	**29**
3	6	9	12	**15**	**18**	**21**	**24**
1	2	4	7	**11**	**16**	**22**	**29**
10	14	18	22	**26**	**30**	**34**	**38**
30	28	26	24	**22**	**20**	**18**	**16**
0	7	14	21	**28**	**35**	**42**	**49**
40	35	30	25	**20**	**15**	**10**	**5**
1	2	4	8	**16**	**32**	**64**	**128**
20	17	14	11	**8**	**5**	**2**	**–1**
60	52	44	36	**28**	**20**	**12**	**4**

Making Patterns

Make up your own number patterns.

1. Keep multiplying the number by 2
1 2 4 8 16 32 64 128

2. Add 11 to the previous number
0 **11 22 33 44 55 66 77**

3. Multiply by 2 and add 1
1 **3 7 15 31 63 127 255**

4. Start with 5 and keep adding 9
5 **14 23 32 41 50 59 68**

5. Start with 100 and take 13 off each number
100 **87 74 61 48 35 22 9**

6. Start with 800 and keep dividing by 2
800 **400 200 100 50 25 12.5 6.25**

7. Start with 0 and keep adding your age
0 **14 28 42 56 70 84 98**

Example

Spot the Rule

The boxes below carry out an operation on the number going into them. Discover this operation and find the missing numbers coming out.

IN	OUT
1	2
2	4
3	6
4	8
5	**10**
6	**12**

Out = In x 2

IN	OUT
1	4
2	7
3	10
4	**13**
5	16
6	**19**

Out = In x 3 + 1

IN	OUT
1	3
2	7
3	11
4	**15**
5	**19**
6	23

Out = In x 4 – 1

IN	OUT
1	7
2	12
3	17
4	22
5	**27**
6	**32**

Out = In x 5 + 2

Rule Boxes

The boxes below carry out an operation on the number going into them. Discover this operation and find the missing numbers coming out.

IN	OUT
1	½
2	1
3	1½
4	**2**
5	**2½**
6	**3**

Out = In x ½

IN	OUT
1	1½
2	2
3	2½
4	**3**
5	3½
10	**6**

Out = In x ½ + 1

IN	OUT
1	8
2	13
3	18
4	23
5	**28**
10	**53**

Out = In x 5 + 3

IN	OUT
1	2
2	9
3	16
4	**23**
5	**30**
8	51

Out = In x 7 – 5

Building Patterns 1

Use matchsticks to build up the pattern below. Extend this pattern up to 6 squares and fill in the table.

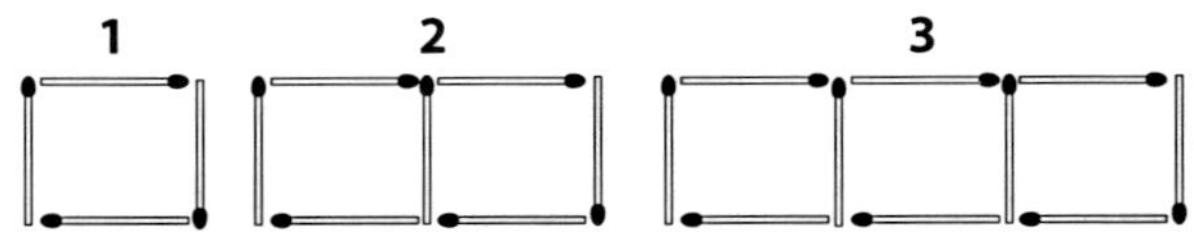

Is there a rule to decide match numbers for any number of squares?

Number of squares	1	2	3	4	5	6
Number of sticks	4	7	10	**13**	**16**	**19**
Rule	**Sticks = 3 x squares + 1**					

How many matches would be needed to make 100 squares? **Sticks = 3 x 100 + 1 = 301**
(Use the rule to work this out).

Building Patterns 2

Use matchsticks to build up the pattern below. Extend the patterns up to 6 side lengths and fill in the table below.

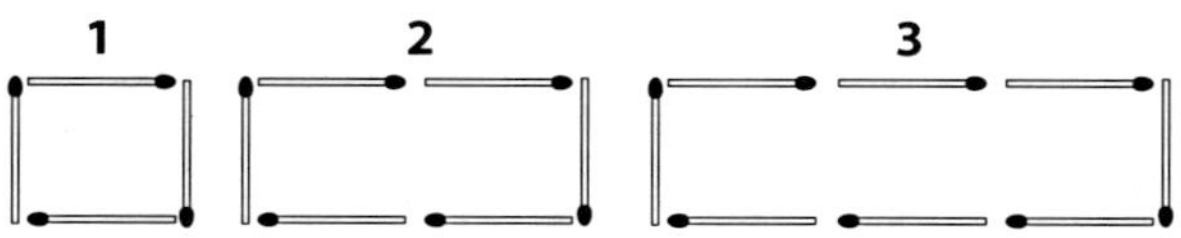

Is there a rule you can use to work out matches needed to make a particular side length?

Length of side	1	2	3	4	5	6
Number of sticks	**4**	**6**	**8**	**10**	**12**	**14**
Rule	**Sticks = 2 x side length + 2**					

For 10 side lengths **22** matches are needed
For 30 side lengths **62** matches are needed
For 100 side lengths **202** matches are needed

Building Patterns 3

Use matchsticks to build up the pattern below. Extend the patterns up to 6 side lengths and fill in the table below.

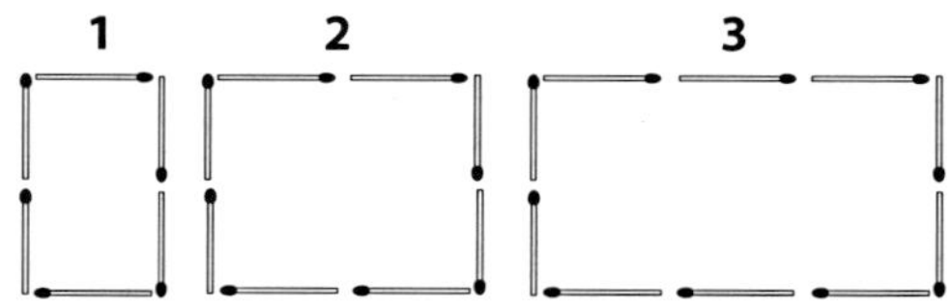

Is there a rule you can use to work out matches needed to make a particular side length?

Length of side	1	2	3	4	5	6
Number of sticks	**6**	**8**	**10**	**12**	**14**	**16**
Rule	**Sticks = 2 x side length + 4**					

For 20 side lengths **44** matches are needed
For 45 side lengths **94** matches are needed
For 100 side lengths **204** matches are needed

Using Rules 1

General expressions provide us with a way of saying what operation we are performing on a set of numbers.

Example
General Expression **(n + 4)**
when n is 1, 2, 3, 4, etc.

N	N + 4
1	5
2	6
3	7
4	8

Try the expression (2n + 1)

N	2N + 1
1	**3**
2	**5**
3	**7**
4	**9**

Using Rules 2

General expressions. Fill in the tables below.

N	N + 2
1	**3**
2	**4**
3	**5**
4	**6**
5	**7**

N	2 N
1	**2**
2	**4**
3	**6**
4	**8**
10	**20**

N	3N + 1
1	**4**
2	**7**
3	**10**
4	**13**
10	**31**

N	3N – 1
1	**2**
2	**5**
3	**8**
4	**11**
10	**29**

Using Rules 3

General expressions. Fill in the tables below.

N	5N + 2
1	**7**
2	**12**
3	**17**
4	**22**
10	**52**

N	N^2
1	**1**
2	**4**
3	**9**
4	**16**
10	**100**

N	4N
1	**4**
2	**8**
3	**12**
4	**16**
8	**32**

N	6N – 5
1	**1**
2	**7**
3	**13**
4	**19**
7	**37**

Using Rules 4

General expressions. Fill in the tables below.

N	2N + 10
1	**12**
2	**14**
3	**16**
4	**18**
20	**50**

N	$N^2 - 1$
1	**0**
2	**3**
3	**8**
4	**15**
10	**99**

N	$N^2 - N$
1	**0**
2	**2**
3	**6**
4	**12**
10	**90**

You invent a rule!

N	Eg. 7n – 4
1	**3**
2	**10**
3	**17**
4	**24**
10	**66**

More Sequences

Find the first 6 terms and the 10th term of the following expressions.

	n=1	n=2	n=3	n=4	n=5	n=6	n=10
n + 4	**5**	**6**	**7**	**8**	**9**	**10**	**14**
2 x n	**2**	**4**	**6**	**8**	**10**	**12**	**20**
3n	**3**	**6**	**9**	**12**	**15**	**18**	**30**
2n + 1	**3**	**5**	**7**	**9**	**11**	**13**	**21**
2n – 1	**1**	**3**	**5**	**7**	**9**	**11**	**19**
n^2	**1**	**4**	**9**	**16**	**25**	**36**	**100**
4n	**4**	**8**	**12**	**16**	**20**	**24**	**40**
2n + 5	**7**	**9**	**11**	**13**	**15**	**17**	**25**
10n	**10**	**20**	**30**	**40**	**50**	**60**	**100**
10n – 10	**0**	**10**	**20**	**30**	**40**	**50**	**90**
$\frac{n}{2}$	$\frac{1}{2}$	**1**	$1\frac{1}{2}$	**2**	$2\frac{1}{2}$	**3**	**5**

Perimeters 1

Find expressions for the perimeters of the shapes below.

1.
P = **a+b+a+b = 2a + 2b**

If a = 3, b = 5
Perimeter is **16**
If a = 7, b = 10
Perimeter is **34**

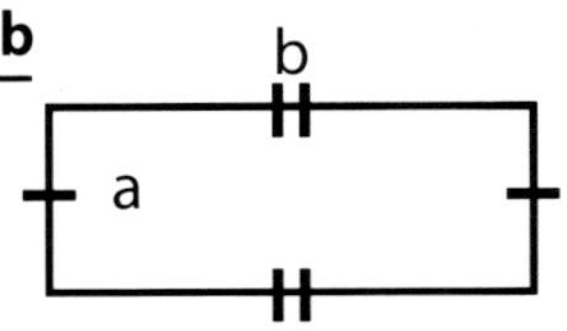

2.
P = **a+a+a+a = 4a**

If a = 11
Perimeter is **44**
If a = 8
Perimeter is **32**

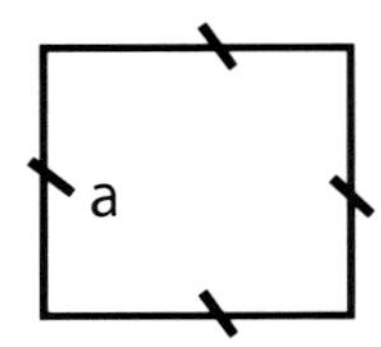

3.
P = **a+a+a = 3a**

If a = 3
Perimeter is **9**

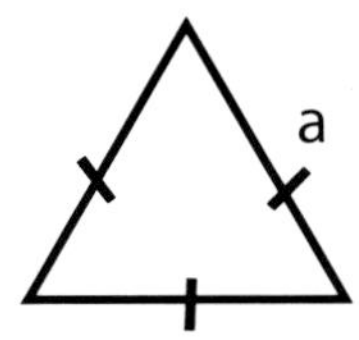

Perimeters 2

Find expressions for the perimeters (P) of the shapes below.

1.
P = **b+b+a+a+a+a+a+a**
P = 2b + 6a units

If a = 2, b = 6
P = **2x6+6x2 = 24**
If a = 7, b = 21
P = **2x21+6x7 = 84**

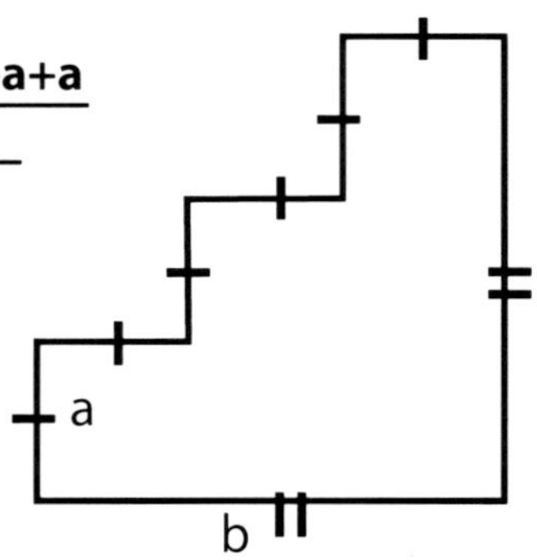

2.
P = **2c+2b+2a units**

If a = 2, b = 4, c = 6
P = **12+8+4 = 24**
If a = 6, b = 10, c = 16
P = **32+20+12 = 64**

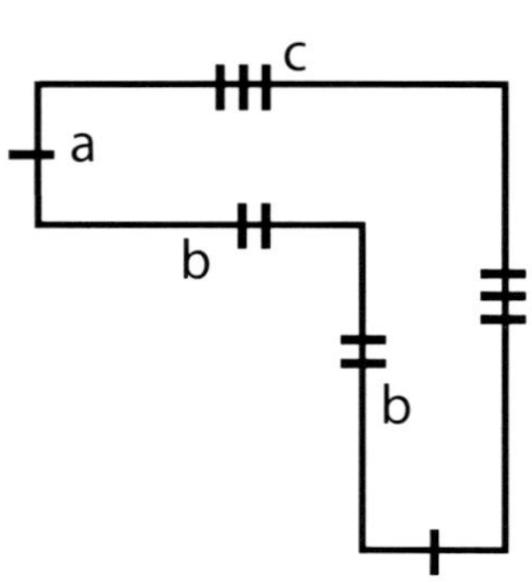

Perimeters 3

Find a number of values for the variables x and y if the perimeter is always 30 cm.

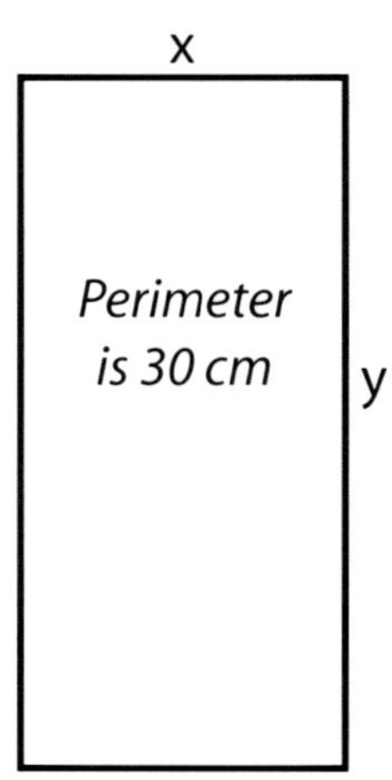

Examples

x	y	x	y
1	14	6	9
2	13	7	8
3	12	8	7
4	11	9	6
5	10	10	5

Rectangle Variables

A rectangle has a perimeter of 40 m. The length and breadth can vary but the perimeter must stay 40 m.

Can you think of some lengths and widths?

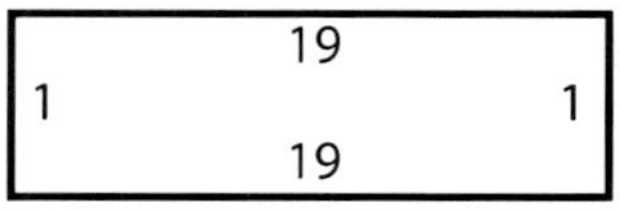

Length	Width	Length	Width
19	**1**	**13**	**7**
18	**2**	**12**	**8**
17	**3**	**11**	**9**
16	**4**	**10**	**10**
15	**5**		

Algebra Rules

Let 'a' represent any number. Find an expression for each of the following.

1. 5 times the number **5a or 5 x a**

2. That number plus 4 **a + 4**

3. That number squared $\mathbf{a^2}$

4. The square root of the number $\sqrt{a}$

5. 3 times the number plus 1 **3a + 1**

6. That number from 100 **100 – a**

7. Half that number **a ÷ 2**

8. That number less 2 **a – 2**

9. That number multiplied by the next consecutive number **a x (a+1)**

10. A quarter of that number **a ÷ 4**

Rewriting Rules

Can you write these expressions in a different way? ***Examples***

1. a + a + a + a = **4 x a = 4a**

2. y + y + y + y = **4 x y = 4y**

3. 3 x a = **a + a + a**

4. a + b + a + b + a + b + a = **4a + 3b**

5. d + e + f + e + e + d = **2d + 3e + f**

6. 3 x a + 2b = **a + a + a + b + b**

7. w + z + y + y = **w + z + 2y**

8. n + m + n + m + 4 = **2n + 2m + 4**

9. 4 x b = **b + b + b + b**

10. 4 x b – 7 = **b + b + b + b – 7**

11. 4 x b -7 + b = **b + b + b + b + b – 7**

12. 6f = **f + f + f + f + f + f**

13. 2f + 3q = **f + f + q + q + q**

More Expressions

Write an expression for these.

1. Add 4 to the product of 3 and 6
4 + (3 x 6)

2. Take 20 from the square of 12
$\mathbf{12^2 - 20}$

3. Multiply the sum of 15 and 21 by 16
(15 + 21) x 16

4. Take 11 from the product of a and b
(a x b) – 11

5. Divide 6 by a and add 7
(6 ÷ a) + 7

6. Multiply a and b and c together
a x b x c or a b c

7. The difference between 28 and d
28 – d

Note: The brackets are solved first.

Larger Triangle

The triangle has sides of 5, 7 and 10 cm. If you increase side 1 by x cm, side 2 by y cm and side 3 by z cm, what would the perimeter of the new triangle be?

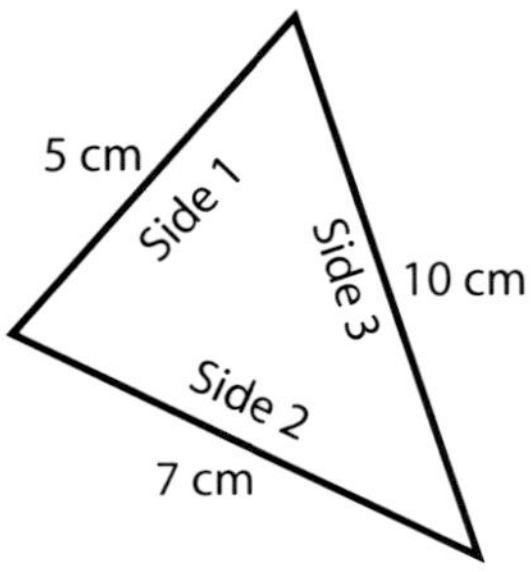

Draw the new triangle and write the expression for its perimeter below.

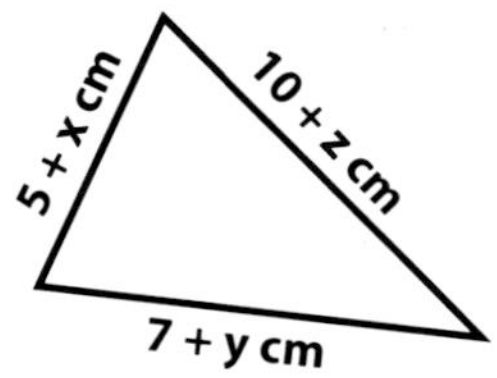

Perimeter will be
5 + x + 7 + y + 10 + z
= 22 + x + y + z cm

Perimeter and Area

Write down the perimeter of this rectangle.

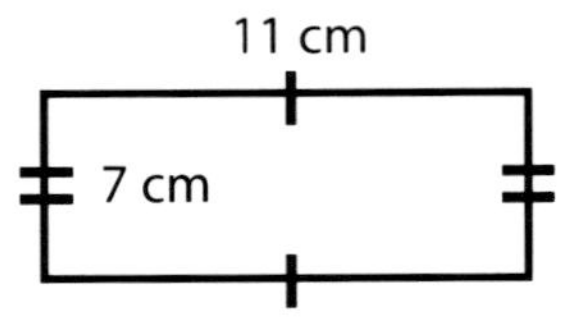

11 + 7 + 11 + 7 = 36 cm

Increase the 11 cm side by 'a' cm and the 7 cm side by 'b' cm.

Write an expression for the new perimeter. **Perimeter will be**
11 + a + 7 + b + 11 + a + 7 + b
= 36 + 2a + 2b

Write an expression for the area of the new triangle.

Area = Length x width
= (11+a) (7+b) = 77 + 7a + 11b + ab cm

Collecting Terms

Collect the like terms below.

1. a + a + a + a + 1	=	**4a + 1**
2. x + 2x + 7x + x	=	**11 x**
3. a + 2b + 5a + b + c	=	**6a + 3b + c**
4. w + w + w + w + y	=	**4w + y**
5. 2x + 10x + y + 4y	=	**12x + 5y**
6. 4y + z + 11y + 3y	=	**18y + z**
7. 12x – x - 4x + 4	=	**7x + 4**
8. a + 2b + c + 8a + 7c	=	**9a +2b + 8c**
9. 46b + 18c – 17a + 6	=	**46b + 18c – 17a + 6**
10. 17x – 5x + 7y + 10y	=	**12x + 17y**
11. 11m – 2m + 18n – 9n	=	**9m + 9n**
12. 7x + 9y – 7y – 3y	=	**7x – 1y**
13. 20b – 8b – 8b – 4b	=	**0**
14. 246y – 23x + 10y	=	**256y – 23x**

Ungrouping

info *The area of the card here can be written as*

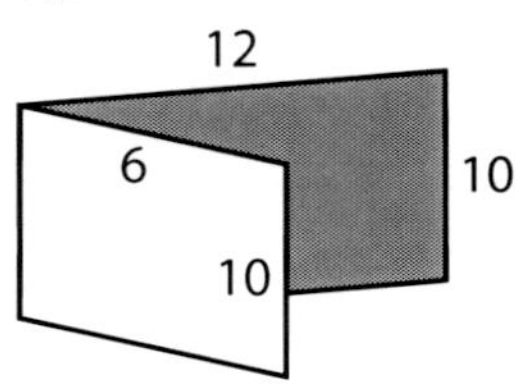

10(6 + 12)
= 10 x 6 + 10 x 12
= 60 + 120
= 180 cm²

Remove the grouping symbols below.

1. 9(8 + 6)	=	**9 x 8 + 9 x 6 = 72 + 54 = 126**
2. 3(a + b)	=	**3a + 3b**
3. 4(x + 8)	=	**4x + 32**
4. a(b + c)	=	**ab + ac**
5. 7(3x + 5)	=	**21x + 35**
6. 10(b + b)	=	**10b + 10b = 20b**

Easier Expressions

One way to remove brackets that group things is shown below.

$2(x + 2y)$ means
$(x + 2y) + (x + 2y)$
$= x + 2y + x + 2y$
$= 2x + 4y$

An easier way is to multiply everything in the bracket by the number or letter outside the bracket, as follows.

$2(x + 2y) = 2x + 4y$

Simplify the following.

$7(3x + 2y) =$ **$21x + 14y$**

$3(5 + 4x) =$ **$15 + 12x$**

Removing Brackets

Remove the brackets and collect like terms.

1. $6(2x + y + z)$ = **$12x + 6y + 6z$**
2. $5(10a + 3b)$ = **$50a + 15b$**
3. $10(2d + x + 5k)$ = **$20d + 10x + 50k$**
4. $\frac{1}{2}(4a + 6b)$ = **$2a + 3b$**
5. $7(4x + 6y)$ = **$28x + 42y$**
6. $a(b + c)$ = **$ab + ac$**
7. $4z(2y + x)$ = **$8yz + 4zx$**
8. $3(a + b) + 4(a + c)$ = **$3a + 3b + 4a + 4c = 7a + 3b + 4c$**
9. $4x + 3(5x + 2y)$ = **$4x + 15x + 6y = 19x + 6y$**
10. $3(2t + 3) + 11(4t + 1)$ = **$6t + 9 + 44t + 11 = 50t + 20$**
11. $6(a + b + c) + 11b$ = **$6a + 6b + 6c + 11b = 6a + 17b + 6c$**

Sorting Expressions

Simplify these expressions by including brackets.

1. $2a + 2b$ = **$2(a + b)$**
2. $6x + 12y + 18$ = **$6(x + 2y + 3)$**
3. $2a + 2b + 2c$ = **$2(a + b + c)$**
4. $3x + 6y$ = **$3(x + 2y)$**
5. $5c + 15d + 10e$ = **$5(c + 3d + 2e)$**
6. $7a + 28$ = **$7(a + 4)$**
7. $12 + 6a$ = **$6(2 + a)$**
8. $ab + 6a$ = **$a(b + 6)$**
9. $5g + g$ = **$g(5 + 1) = 6g$**
10. $60a + 120ac$ = **$60a(1 + 2c)$**
11. $4ab + 2ab$ = **$2ab(2 + 1) = 6ab$**
12. $ad + d$ = **$d(a + 1)$**
13. $3p + 6m + 18n$ = **$3(p + 2m + 6n)$**

Solving Equations

Solve the following equations by finding the number x.

1. $x + 2 = 6$ **$x = 6 - 2 = 4$**
2. $x - 8 = 10$ **$x = 18$**
3. $x \div 3 = 4$ **$x = 12$**
4. $x^2 = 16$ **$x = 4$**
5. $3x = 9$ **$x = 3$**
6. $2x + 1 = 5$ **$x = 2$**
7. $2x + 1 = 7$ **$x = 3$**
8. $2x + 1 = 9$ **$x = 4$**
9. $\sqrt{x} = 4$ **$x = 16$**
10. $x + 8 = 24$ **$x = 16$**
11. $x^2 + 1 = 26$ **$x = 5$**
12. $x \div 5 = 6$ **$x = 30$**
13. $x^2 = 49$ **$x = 7$**
14. $6x = 60$ **$x = 10$**

Toss a Coin

info

- ***Statistics*** *involves collecting and displaying data.*
- ***Predictions*** *involve the analysis of data resulting in educated guesses as to what will happen in future or under different circumstances.*
- *When we try to predict the chance of something happening we are dealing with* ***probability****.*

If you toss a coin 40 times, what is the predicted tally of heads and tails?
Try it out and record your results below.

Outcome	Tally *Example*	Total
Head	𝍸 𝍸 𝍸 II	17
Tail	𝍸 𝍸 𝍸 𝍸 III	23

Do your results fit your prediction? Exactly? Approximately? ______________________

____

Toss 2 Coins

Toss two coins 40 times and record the results below. You can tick numbers 1 to 40 to keep count.
Note: you can observe a HH, HT, or TH outcome (H is heads, T is tails).
Example

~~1~~	~~2~~	~~3~~	~~4~~	~~5~~	~~6~~	~~7~~	~~8~~	~~9~~	~~10~~
~~11~~	~~12~~	~~13~~	~~14~~	~~15~~	~~16~~	~~17~~	~~18~~	~~19~~	~~20~~
~~21~~	~~22~~	~~23~~	~~24~~	~~25~~	~~26~~	~~27~~	~~28~~	~~29~~	~~30~~
~~31~~	~~32~~	~~33~~	~~34~~	~~35~~	~~36~~	~~37~~	~~38~~	~~39~~	~~40~~

Outcome	Tally	Frequency
HH	𝍸 𝍸	10
HT	𝍸 𝍸 𝍸 III	18
TT	𝍸 𝍸 II	12

Are the results as you would predict?

____

____

Throwing Dice

Throw a dice 100 times and record the results below.
Example

Number	Tally	Total
1	𝍸 𝍸 II	12
2	𝍸 𝍸 𝍸	15
3	𝍸 𝍸 𝍸 𝍸 II	22
4	𝍸 𝍸 III	13
5	𝍸 𝍸 𝍸 III	18
6	𝍸 𝍸 𝍸 𝍸	20

Record the dice throw **data** on the graph below.

Example

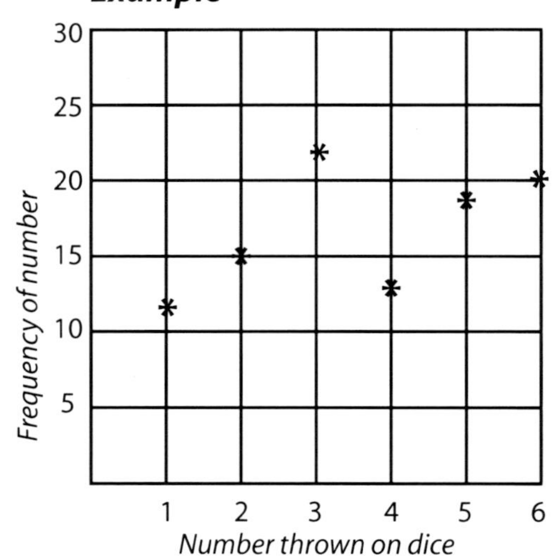

Is this what you expected?

____

____

2 Dice Game

Roll two dice 40 times. Each time.
Add the numbers on the two dice and make a mark in the 'Tally' column next to the number that they add up to.
After 40 throws, count up the total tally.

Number	Tally	Total
1		0
2	||	2
3	||	2
4	|	1
5	|||	3
6	𝍸 ||	7
7	𝍸 𝍸	10
8	𝍸	5
9	||||	4
10	|||	3
11	|	1
12	||	2

Why do you think some of the totals are most 'popular'?
More chances of rolling these.

Did you ever get a total of 1?
No

Card Cut

Take turns to randomly draw a card from a full pack of playing cards placed face down. Keep a tally of how many hearts, clubs, diamonds and spades you pick up. Repeat 50 times.

Suit		Tally	Total
Heart	♥	𝍸 𝍸 𝍸	15
Club	♣	𝍸 𝍸	10
Diamond	◆	𝍸 𝍸 |||	13
Spade	♠	𝍸 𝍸 ||	12

At the end, sort the pack into suits and count how many cards are in each suit. Would you have expected the above result? **Yes.**
Equal chance of picking any suit, so total for each suit is approximately the same.

Probability Words

We use many different words to describe the probability or chance of things happening.

Here are two examples of words that we use.

1. There is a good chance it will rain today.
2. The odds are in favour of the horse winning the race.

Write down some more words that you would use to talk about probability.

Examples

3. It's a fifty-fifty chance that Derek says something stupid.
4. You will never get this problem right.
5. Somebody will spot me doing this for sure.
6. There is a slim chance that the book sale is still on.

Measuring Chance

info

If something is certain to happen we give it a probability of 1.
If it cannot happen we give it a value of 0.

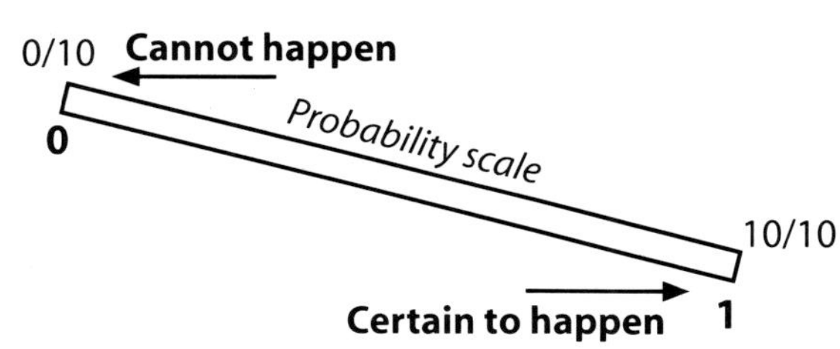

Estimate the chance of the following happening as a fraction out of 10.	
It will rain today	**2/10**
You will go to bed today	**10/10 or 1**
An alien will land in the garden	**0/10**
A friend will phone you	**8/10**
You will be given homework	**7/10**
You will be given a job to do at home	**10/10**

Picking a Lollie

g = Green
y = Yellow
r = Red
w = White
b = Blue
p = Pink

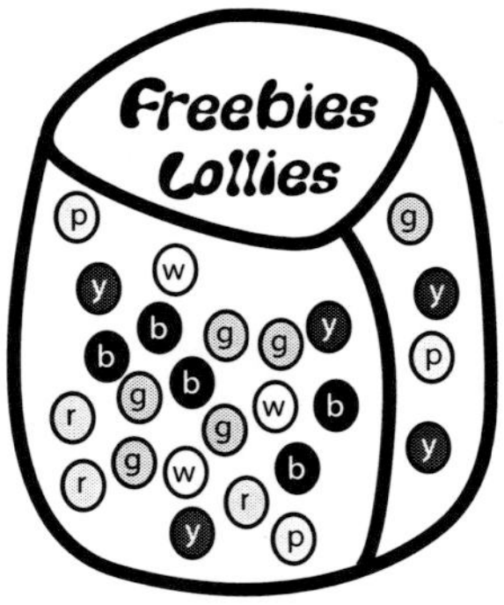

There are 25 lollies in this bag.

What is the probability of picking out the following?

A Green lolly	**6/25**	A Red lolly	**3/25**
A Yellow lolly	**5/25**	A White lolly	**3/25**
A Blue lolly	**5/25**	A Pink lolly	**3/25**

Dice Numbers

Throw a dice 60 times. Record the number that turns up each time on the tally sheet. Add up your final tally for each number.

Number	Tally *Example*	Total
1	卌 卌 卌 卌 卌 II	27
2	卌 卌 卌 卌 卌 卌 III	33
3	卌 卌 卌 卌 II	22
4	卌 卌 II	12
5	卌 卌 卌 卌 卌 III	28
6	zero! *(is this possible)?*	0

Example

In theory, what is the probability of any one number turning up? **1/6**

Does your tally agree with the theory exactly? ______

Why not? ______

______

Choosing Colours

Put 10 red counters
+ 5 blue counters
+ 2 yellow counters into a bag

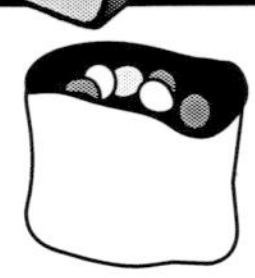

What is the probability of drawing a red **10/17**
What is the probability of drawing blue **5/17**
What is the probability of drawing yellow **2/17**

Without looking pick out a counter 60 times, making sure you put it back in the bag each time. Each time, record the colour on the sheet below. Add up the totals.

Example

Colour	Tally	Frequency
Red	卌 卌 卌 卌 卌 卌 IIII	34
Blue	卌 卌 卌 III	18
Yellow	卌 III	8

Are these results expected? Exactly? Approximately? ______

______

______

Dice Probability

Imagine you are rolling a dice. What is the probability of rolling each of the following?

Write your answers as fractions.

Roll	Probability
A one	**1/6**
An even number	**3/6 or 1/2**
An odd number	**3/6 or 1/2**
A number less than 3	**2/6 or 1/3**
A multiple of 3	**2/6 or 1/3**
A number greater than 4	**2/6 or 1/3**
Any number but 4	**5/6**
A seven	**0/6**

Choosing Cards

Work out the probability of choosing the following from a full pack of 52 cards. Write your answers as fractions.

Any Heart	13/52	An even number	20/52
Any Ace	4/52	A red card	26/52
A Club	13/52	Any card above 10 (Aces Low!)	12/52
A Jack	4/52	A picture card	12/52
A Jack of clubs	1/52	A black card	26/52
A 3 of any suit	4/52	Any King	4/52
A 3 of Diamonds	1/52	A card between 5 and 8 (6 or 7)	8/52
A Queen	4/52	A Queen or King	8/52

Predicting Spin

You can spin the arrow around on the following circular board.

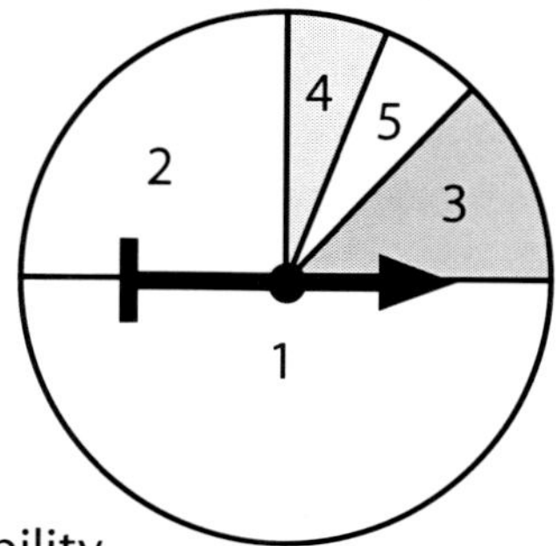

What is the probability of getting the following numbers? Write your answers as fractions.

1	1/2	4	1/16
2	1/4	5	1/16
3	1/8		

How many spins would you expect to make before you spin a 4? **16 perhaps. In fact though you have a better-than-even chance of having got a 4 after 11 spins (too complicated to explain why here!)**

Dice Combinations

If you roll 2 dice and add the total of the 2 numbers that you get, what is the probability of getting various different totals?

Fill in the grid below to help you work this out.

Dice 1 →, *Dice 2* ↓

	1	2	3	4	5	6
1	2	3	4	5	6	7
2	3	4	5	6	7	8
3	4	5	6	7	8	9
4	5	6	7	8	9	10
5	6	7	8	9	10	11
6	7	8	9	10	11	12

Probability of a **2** 1/36 **3** 2/36 **4** 3/36

5 4/36 **6** 5/36 **7** 6/36 **8** 5/36

9 4/36 **10** 3/36 **11** 2/36 **12** 1/36

Alphabet Chance

You close you eyes and randomly point to a letter of the alphabet.

A	B	C	D	E	F	G
H	I	J	K	L	M	N
O	P	Q	R	S	T	U
V	W	X	Y	Z		

What is the probability of pointing to:

- a vowel **5/26**
- the letter **L** **1/26**
- a consonant **21/26**
- any letter in the word **PROBABILITY** **9/26**
- any letter in your name **How many different letters/26**

Surveys

info ***Surveys** involve collecting data.*

Think of 6 different groups of people or organisations that might use data.

Examples **police**

newspaper

advertisers

car makers

governments

teachers

Think of 3 things that you could survey at school. ***Examples***

Good and bad school rules

T.V. programmes

Entertainment venues

Sampling

info *A **census** involves a survey of a whole population.*

*A survey of a **random sample** of a population involves a small fraction of the total population. The people (or things) involved should be chosen randomly, which means that every person (or item) in the population should have an equal chance of being chosen. Certain groups are not given preference.* ***Examples***

How could you get a random sample of:

1. Supermarket Shoppers? **Pick every 50th customer.**

2. Library users? **A survey put in the mail to a random range of customers.**

Food Survey

Write down the name of 2 popular foods allowed for sale at the canteen.

1. Food ***Example*** **Hamburgers**
   Results 卌 卌 卌 卌 卌 ||

2. Food **Hot chips**
   Results 卌 卌 卌 卌 |||

Ask class members which they prefer. For each answer you get, put a tally mark next to the preferred food above.

Discuss the results with the rest of the group. How would you go about doing a food survey for the whole school?

Taking a Tally

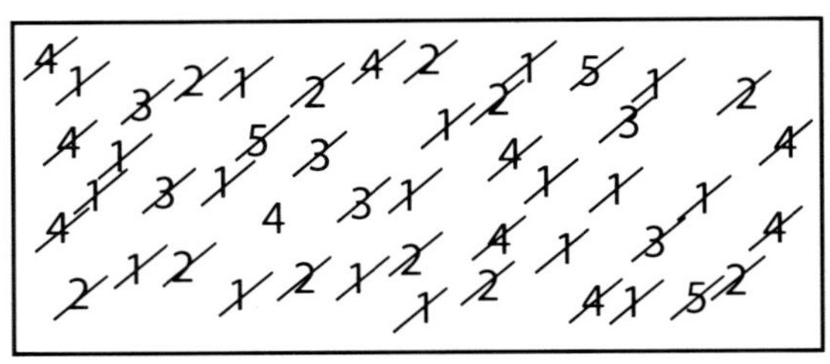

Count how many times each number occurs above. As you count each number, cross it off and make a mark next to that number in the tally sheet below.
Which number turns up most often?

Number	Tally	Total
1	卌 卌 卌 |||	**18**
2	卌 卌		**11**
3	卌		**6**
4	卌 卌	**10**
5	|||	**3**

Use of Letters

Investigate which letters are used most commonly.

To do this, count the letters used in the paragraph below. For each letter, make a mark in the tally sheet alongside *(keep your tally strokes small)*.
To help with the counting, each time you reach a total of 5 record it as:

| = one || = two ||| = three |||| = four 𝍸 = five

> "Once there were four children whose names were Peter, Susan, Edmund and Lucy. This story is about something that happened to them when they were sent away from London during the war because of air raids."

Quote from "The Lion, the Witch and the Wardrobe" by C.S. Lewis.

Count up the total for each letter.
Which letters are the most common?
E T N R H A

Which letters are not used at all?
J K Q V X Z

	Tally	Total		Tally	Total
a	𝍸 𝍸 ||	**12**	n	𝍸 𝍸 |||	**13**
b	||	**2**	o	𝍸 𝍸 |	**11**
c	||||	**4**	p	|||	**3**
d	𝍸 |||	**8**	q		**0**
e	𝍸 𝍸 𝍸 𝍸 𝍸 |	**26**	r	𝍸 𝍸 |||	**13**
f	|||	**3**	s	𝍸 𝍸 |	**11**
g	||	**2**	t	𝍸 𝍸 ||||	**14**
h	𝍸 𝍸 ||	**12**	u	𝍸 ||	**7**
i	𝍸 ||	**7**	v		**0**
j		**0**	w	𝍸 ||	**7**
k		**0**	x		**0**
l	|||	**3**	y	||||	**4**
m	𝍸	**5**	z		**0**

Sorting and Presenting Data

A class of 30 gets the following results in a test out of 10. Take a tally of the results and construct a line graph of the results on the grid alongside.

3	7	6	5	7	6
6	7	8	9	10	8
9	6	5	7	4	7
4	7	3	6	8	5
7	6	7	8	7	4

Score	Tally	Score	Tally
1	**0**	6	𝍸 |
2	**0**	7	𝍸 ||||
3	||	8	||||
4	|||	9	||
5	|||	10	|

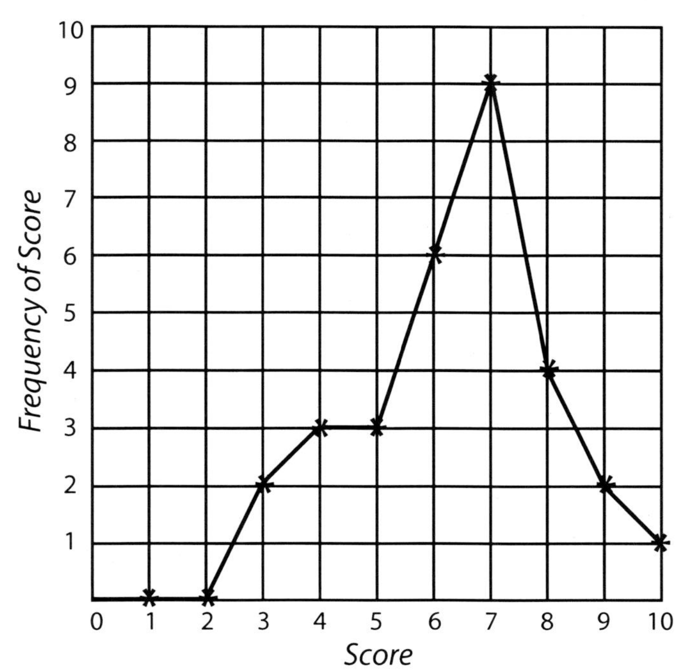

What was the most common score? **7**
What was the highest score? **10**

Picture Graphs 1

info *Using **picture graphs** is an easy and fun way to display data.*

Pies sold at a school canteen

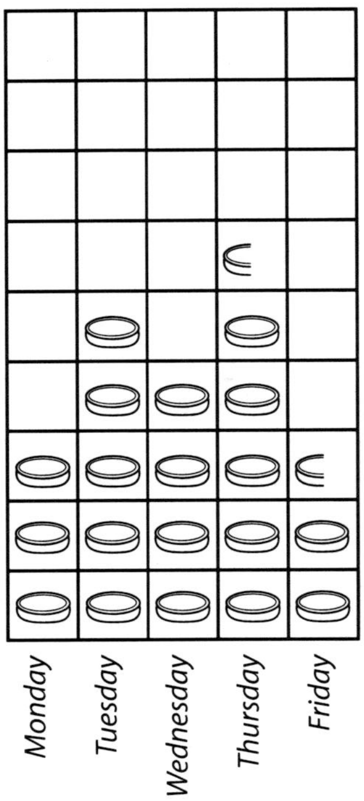

Scale:
=10 pies

How many were sold on:

Mon **30**

Tue **50**

Wed **40**

Thur **55**

Fri **25**

What was the week's total?

200

Picture Graphs 2

Movies hired out at a video shop

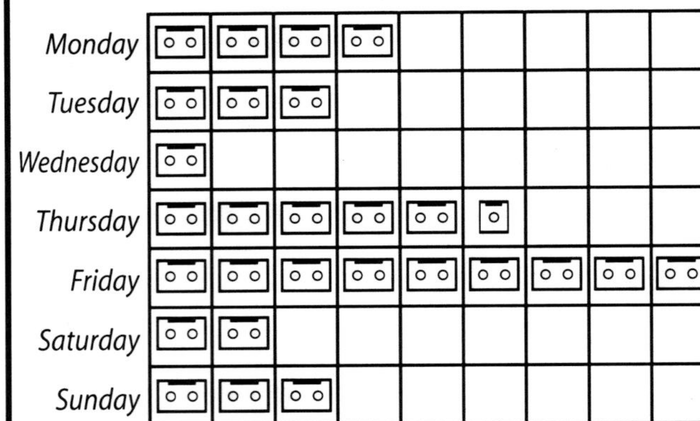

Scale: = 20 videos = 10 videos

How many were hired over the week?

550

What day were most videos hired?

Friday

Why so few hired on Wednesday?

Midweek/work

Why so few on Saturday?

Various answers

Pie Graph 1

A day at Camp Fabulous

Scale: Each sector represents 1 hour.

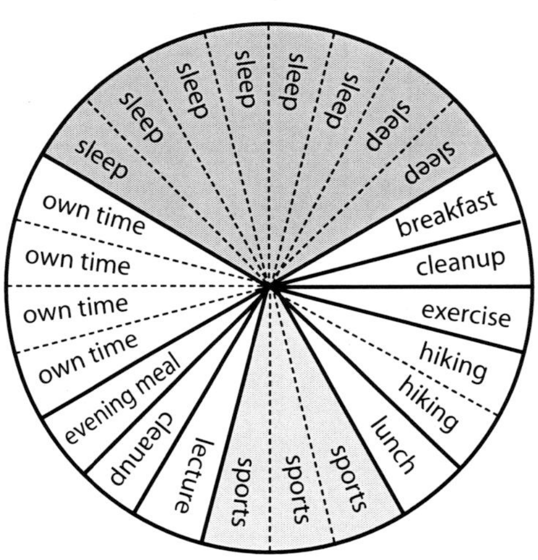

How long were you allowed to sleep? **8hrs**

How much time was given to hiking? **2hrs**

How much time was allowed for eating? **3hrs**

How much time was spent in cleaning up? **2hrs**

How much 'own' time was permitted? **4hrs**

Pie Graph 2

Use the Pie Graph to display how you spend your day. It is divided up into 1 hour sectors.

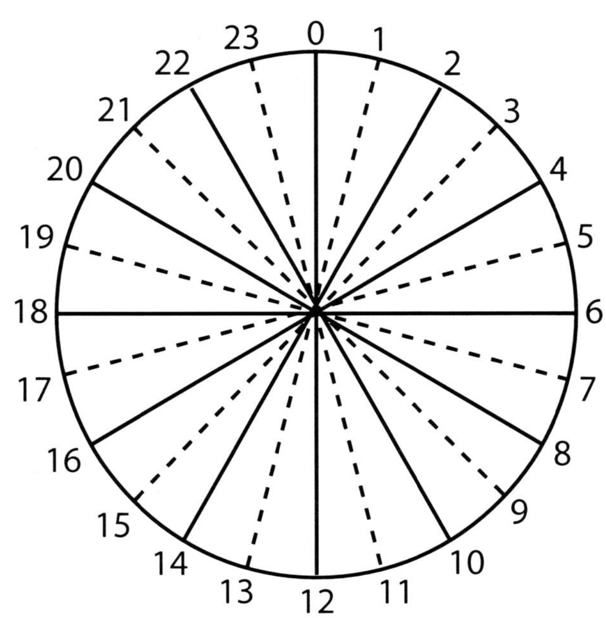

Will be individual for each person.

Bar Chart

An entire school of 900 students filled in a census on how they got to school on one particular day. The results are displayed in the a bar graph below.

Methods of travel

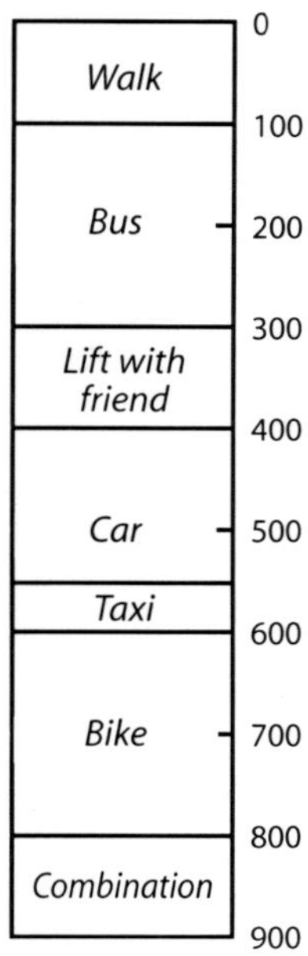

How many walked? **100**

Did more people use a bus in preference to a car? **Yes**

How many used taxis? **50**

Were there more walkers than bikers? **No**

Column Graph

info *__Column graphs__ have a title, 2 axes and labels.*

Number of books read in a year

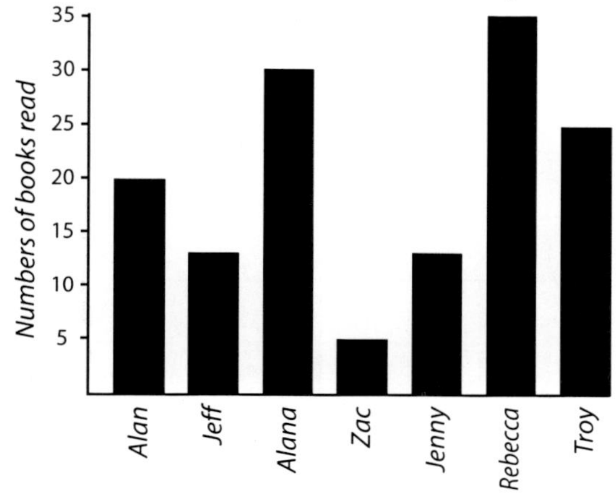

Who read the least? **Zac**

Who read 20 books? **Alan**

Who read the same amount as each other? **Jeff and Jenny**

What was the total number of books read by all? **20+13+30+5+13+35+25 = 141**

Histogram

info *__Histograms__ are column graphs with no spaces between columns.*

Questions answered incorrectly in the competition

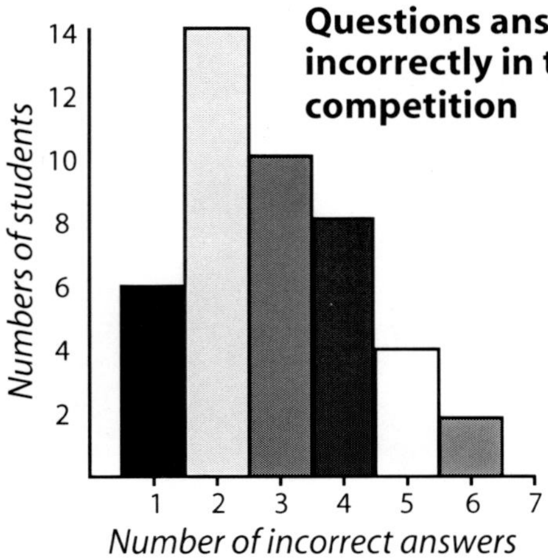

How many answered 4 incorrectly? **8**

How many made more than 4 mistakes? **6**

How many made less than 3 mistakes? **20**

How many students entered the competition? ***cannot say exactly***

Line Graph

info *__Line graphs__ show lines connecting points.*

Distance travelled on a bike ride

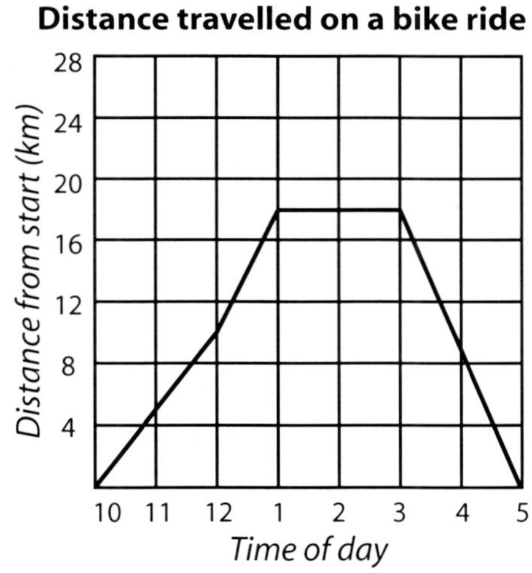

How far was travelled in the first 2 hours? **10 km**

What was the speed in the next hour? **8 km/hr**

How long did the person rest? **2 hrs**

What was the average speed on the return trip? **9 km/hr**

Data Range

info

*The **range** of a set of numbers is the difference between the highest and lowest numbers.*

Find the range of the following.

1.	8	12	16	4	1	17	5	**17 - 1 = 16**
2.	1	3	7	4	2	7	8	**8 - 1 = 7**
3.	76	41	62	19	38	79	5	**79 - 5 = 74**
4.	1.2	6.4	3.7	4.4	7.8	3.5	0.1	**7.8 - 0.1 = 7.7**
5.	0.6	0.4	0.1	1.2	3.3	5.0	4.7	**5.0 - 0.1 = 4.9**
6.	–3	2	4	–1	6	8	–5	**8 - -5 = 13**
7.	–1	–4	–8	–11	–2	–3	–5	**-11 - -1 = 10**
8.	£6	£1	£30	£9	£16	£4	£17	**£30 - £1 = £29**
9.	£0.25	£0.90	£0.80	£0.15				**0.90 - 0.15 = 0.75**
10.	$\frac{1}{15}$	$\frac{3}{15}$	$\frac{12}{15}$	$\frac{8}{15}$	$\frac{6}{15}$	$\frac{5}{15}$	$\frac{11}{15}$	$\mathbf{\frac{12}{15} - \frac{1}{15} = \frac{11}{15}}$

Data Mode

info

*In a collection of data the **mode** is the number that turns up with the highest frequency.*

Find the mode of the following.

1. 6, 2, 9, 2, 5, 5, 2, 4 — **2**

2. 11, 15, 9, 12, 8, 12, 15, 12 — **12**

3. 1, 3, 6, 2, 6, 1, 6, 5, 7, 6 — **6**

4. 3.4, 3.1, 3.2, 3.1, 3.3, 3.5 — **3.1**

5. 112, 116, 113, 113, 110, 112, 113 — **113**

6. $\frac{1}{8}$ $\frac{2}{8}$ $\frac{2}{8}$ $\frac{4}{8}$ $\frac{5}{8}$ $\frac{4}{8}$ $\frac{2}{8}$ $\frac{4}{8}$ $\frac{3}{8}$ — $\mathbf{\frac{2}{8}}$

7. 18, 16, 17, 16, 18, 16, 17, 17, 17 — **17**

8. 981, 980, 979, 980, 981, 980 — **980**

9. 64, 37, 64, 29, 47, 64 — **64**

10. 1, 2, 3, 3, 1, 1, 2, 2, 3, 1, 2, 2 — **2**

Data Median 1

info

*When a collection of data is arranged from largest to smallest or smallest to largest the **median** is the score found in the middle.*

Example 2: 7, 3, 4, 9, 2, 5, 5
is sorted: 2, 3, 4, **5**, 5, 7, 9 giving a median of 5

Example 1: 3, 8, 4, 6, 5, 7
is sorted: 3, 4, **5**, **6**, 7, 8 giving a median of 5.5

Find the median of the following.

1. 4, 2, 3, 4, 5, 6, 9, 4, 6, 2, 5
2, 2, 3, 4, 4, (4,) 5, 5, 6, 6, 9 = 4

2. 13, 8, 17, 19, 11, 14, 7, 12
7, 8, 11, (12, 13,) 14, 17, 19 = 12.5

3. 9, 11, 16, 12, 5, 7, 8, 7, 7
5, 7, 7, 7, (8,) 9, 11, 12, 16 = 8

Data Median 2

Find the median of the following.

1. 6, 4, 3, 5, 5, 7, 8
3, 4, 5, (5,) 6, 7, 8 = 5

2. 24, 26, 25, 26, 25, 25
24, 25, (25, 25,) 26, 26 = 25

3. 0.3, 0.7, 0.5, 0.6, 0.5
0.3, 0.5, (0.5,) 0.6, 0.7 = 0.5

4. 1.5, 1.2, 0.9, 1.4, 1.0, 1.1
0.9, 1.0, (1.1, 1.2,) 1.4, 1.5 = 1.15

5. 107, 124, 111, 117, 119
107, 111, (117,) 119, 124 = 117

6. 34, 58, 68, 51, 59, 70
34, 51, (58, 59,) 68, 70 = 58.5

Data Mean 1

info

*The **mean** of a set of numbers is the average. We get the mean by adding up all the numbers and dividing by the number of numbers that we have.*

Example: Four students obtained scores of 5, 6, 8 and 9 on a test.
There are four numbers, so the average or mean score was
(5 + 6 + 8 + 9) ÷ 4 = 7

Find the mean of 3, 6, 8, 4, 7, 5 and 4

Mean = **3 + 6 + 8 + 4 + 7 + 5 + 4**

= 37/7

Mean = 5.29

Data Mean 2

Find the mean of the following.

1. 4, 7, 8, 1
(4+7+8+1) ÷ 4 = 20 ÷ 4 = 5
2. 6, 9, 10, 7, 5, 8
(6+9+10+7+5+8) ÷ 6 = 45 ÷ 6 = 7.5
3. 3.1, 3.8, 3.6, 3.4
(3.1+ 3.8+3.6+3.4) ÷ 4 = 3.475
4. 62, 51, 58, 49, 55
(62+51+58+49+55) ÷ 5 = 55
5. 19, 23, 28, 21, 23
(19+23+28+21+23) ÷ 5 = 22.8
6. 0.5, 0.6, 0.8, 0.5
(0.5+0.6+0.8+0.5) ÷ 4 = 0.6
7. 13, 16, 14, 17, 8
(13+16+14+17+18) ÷ 5 = 13.6

Data Mean 3

Count the number of items in each of 6 boxes of drawing pins or paper clips. Record the results below and work out the mean.

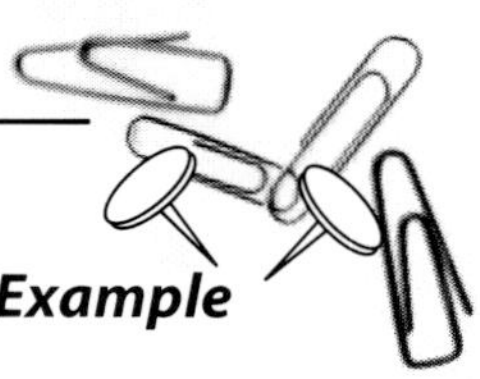

	Contents
Box 1	**98**
Box 2	**97**
Box 3	**102**
Box 4	**103**
Box 5	**100**
Box 6	**100**

Example

Mean =

98 + 97 + 102

+ 103 + 100 + 100

= 600

600 ÷ 6 = 100

Does your figure agree with the "average contents" statement on the box? **Yes**

Analysing Results

Work out a set of 10 questions to put to a group of students. Let the group answer them. Mark the answers.

Example
Record how many were answered correctly here. **8 4 6 9 10 9 8 7 9 7**

What is the **range**? (biggest score – smallest) **10 – 4 = 6**

What is the **mode**? (score repeated most often) **9**

What is the **median**? (in the middle when arranged from smallest to largest) **8**

What is the **mean**? (total divided by number of items) **7.7**

Data Collection and Analysis

Use the sheet below to record up to 35 items of data from any source that you choose. Then work out the range, mode, median and mean.

1. Results ***Example:*** **General Knowledge Quiz. (Out of 50)**

Result	Score	Result	Score
1	**37**	19	**35**
2	**25**	20	**45**
3	**14**	21	**39**
4	**44**	22	**24**
5	**25**	23	**40**
6	**37**	24	**27**
7	**34**	25	**31**
8	**16**	26	**15**
9	**22**	27	**27**
10	**48**	28	**32**
11	**15**	29	**38**
12	**36**	30	**40**
13	**28**	31	**43**
14	**26**	32	
15	**46**	33	
16	**27**	34	
17	**27**	35	
18	**41**		

2. Range
The difference between the lowest and highest score.
48 – 14 = 34

3. Mode
The number that turns up most often.
27 (4 times)

4. Median
The number in the middle when **all** the scores are written down from lowest to highest.

14 15 15 16 22 24 25 25 26 27

27 27 27 28 31 (32) 34 35 36 37 37

38 39 40 40 41 43 44 45 46 48

Median = 32

5. Mean (Average)
The total of all the scores divided by the number of scores (number of data items).

sum of all scores = 984

number of scores = 31

mean = 984 ÷ 31 (2 decimal places)

The Great School Car Park Survey

Do teachers drive gas guzzlers, bombs, sports cars or high performance sedans?
Find out by completing a survey of their cars in the school car park *(but do not touch any of the cars).*

Systematically walk through the car park and make a note of the type of cars. Record how many of each type. ***Example only***

Car Make	Tally	Freq	Car Make	Tally	Freq
Ford	卌 卌 ||	12			
Toyota	卌 ||	7			
Hyundai	|||	3			
VW	|	1			
Subaru	||	2			
Mazda	||||	4			
Daewoo	||	2			
Nissan	||||	4			
Holden	卌	5			
Honda	|||	3			
Mitsubishi	||	2			
Suzuki	|||	3			
Diahatsu	||||	4			
Landrover	|	1			

Remember: Complete a tally using the correct method.

This is correct. 卌 卌 卌 卌 ||

This is not! | | | | \ | / | | | | | \ | / | | | | | | \ | /

You could also collect additional information about each car, for example, the colour, how messy, how clean or how rusty.

Results of the Great Car Park Survey

Use the grid below to draw a graph to present your data.
You can use any type of graph. ***Example***

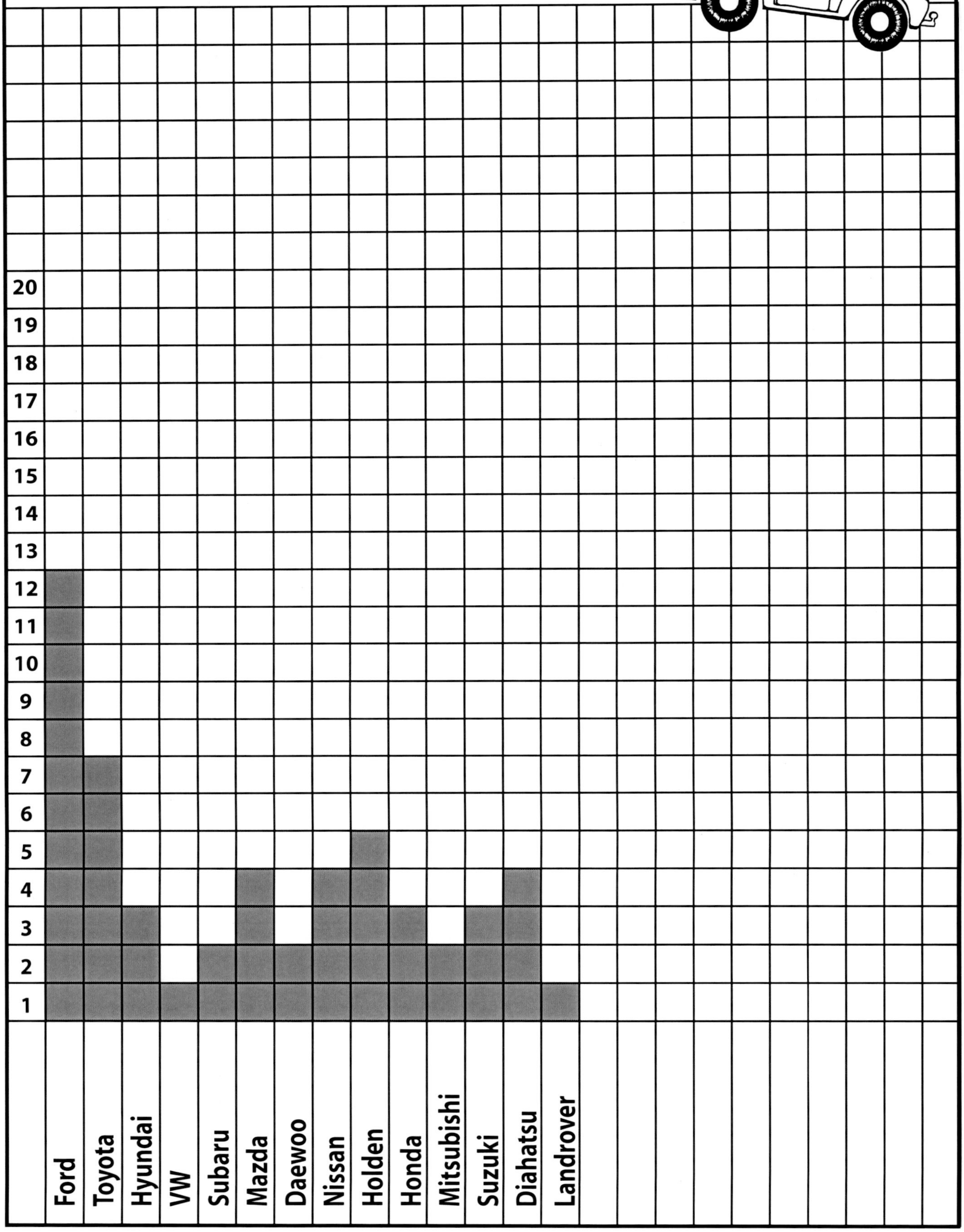

Class Weight Survey

Survey the weight of everyone in the class.

Name (Go by a 'false' name if you prefer!!!)	**Weight (kg)**	**+ or – to show above or below the mean**
Jeff	59	–
Susan	62	–
Aaron	70	+
Nigel	71	+
Marg	60	–
Veronica	57	–
Frank	84	+
Katrina	70	+
Pauline	63	–
Christine	59	–
Malcolm	68	–
David S.	76	+
Lucy	58	–
Brian	61	–
Keith	77	+
Rita	60	–
Eileen	60	–
Gillian	61	–
Steve	86	+
David B	80	+
Robert	73	+
Bill	80	+
Harry	67	–
Sally	54	–
Will	78	+
Bob	86	+
Derek	75	+
Eric	75	+

Mode = **60 kg**

Median = **69 kg**

Mean = **69 kg**

Which student is closest to the mean? **Aaron, Katrina, Malcolm**

MATHS REINFORCERS

ALGEBRA, STATISTICS, PROBABILITY

About this resource…

The four resource books in the **Maths Reinforcers** series are designed for students who are experiencing difficulties with maths, and need extra learning support. The many activities will assist students to build skills and understanding, and are presented in a flexible and easy-to-use format.

The worksheets can be used as quick 'warm ups', as targeted activities for particular students, to engage pairs or small groups, for early finishers, for homework, or for pre and post testing of various competencies.

Answers are provided for self, peer or teacher marking.

Titles in this series are:

Book A - Number Skills

Book B - Fractions, Decimals, Percentages

Book C - Ratio and Proportion, Mass, Time, Plane Shapes, Length, Area, Volume

Book D - Algebra, Statistics, Probability

About the author…

Richard Free is a maths specialist working with students who have difficulty with mathematics.

User Friendly Resources

User Friendly Resources is an educational publishing house which specialises in developing photocopiable books for students, teachers and school leaders. Our resources range across the curriculum and are written by educators for early childhood, primary and secondary schools.

ISBN 1-86968-219-X
9 781869 682194